# Tracing Contours

## Reflections on World Mission and Christianity

# Tracing Contours
## Reflections on World Mission and Christianity

edited by

# Rodney L. Petersen & Marian Gh. Simion

BOSTON THEOLOGICAL INSTITUTE

NEWTON CENTRE, MA 02459

*Tracing Contours: Reflections on World Mission and Christianity*
Rodney L. Petersen, Marian Gh. Simion, editors

First Paperback Edition 2010

 Boston Theological Institute
ISBN 978-0-9843796-1-3


Cover design & artwork: Marian Gh. Simion

21st Century Ministry Booklets ISSN: 1940-7866
ISBN 978-0-9843796-1-3

Printed in the United States of America by Arvest Press, Inc., Waltham, MA.

*with thanks to current and past members of the
International Mission and Ecumenism Faculty Committee
of the schools of the Boston Theological Institute, including:*


**Andover Newton Theological School**
Orlando Costas; Meredith Handspicker; Robert Pazmiño;
Daniel Jeyaraj; Nimi Wariboko

**Boston College, School of Theology and Ministry
(and formerly Weston Jesuit School of Theology)**
Roger Haight, S.J.; Margaret Eletta Guider, OSF

**Boston College, Department of Theology**
Francis X. Clooney, S.J.; Catherine Cornille; Raymond Helmick, S.J.

**Boston University School of Theology**
Dana L. Robert; Imani-Sheila Newsome; Elizabeth Parsons

**Episcopal Divinity School**
Ivan T. Kaufman; Ian T. Douglas; Christopher Duraisingh

**Gordon-Conwell Theological Seminary**
J. Christy Wilson; Kurt Richardson; Peter Kuzmi ;
Tim Tennent; Moonjang Lee; Todd Johnson

**Harvard Divinity School**
Harvey Cox; David Little; Susan Abraham

**Holy Cross Greek Orthodox School of Theology**
George Papademetriou; Timothy Patitsas; Luke Veronis

**Saint John's Seminary**
James Roach; Bryan Hehir; John MacInnis

# Table of Contents

# FOREWORD

Tracing Contours: Reflections on World Mission and Christianity is an anthology of theological reflections published in the *BTI Newsletter* during the past two decades by guests, professors and graduate students of the nine schools of the Boston Theological Institute. For the last quarter century, the *BTI Newsletter* has been a regular feature of the Boston Theological Institute by providing a summary of activity in the schools, while highlighting theological interests and academic programs.

In the period marked by the centennial of the 1910 Edinburgh Missionary Conference, mission has become a matter to ecumenical concern. That conference can arguably be said to have had a profound and continuing impact upon the growing dialogue of Orthodox, Roman Catholic and Protestants over conceptions of mission, in contrast with missionary activities that gave impetus and often reshaped ecumenical and inter-faith discussions.

The intent behind this volume is to offer a glimpse of local creativity that reveals a deep commitment in this consortium to the essence of Christian mission. It also highlights a strong commitment to the concerns of interfaith dialogue and relationships, believing that "we have this treasure in jars of clay" (II Cor. 4:7). Commitments to human flourishing and to mission understood as reconciliation, are themes that continue to surface on communal trajectories, and as necessities of faith in the context of religious freedom and in freedom from fear.

Several themes were followed over the course of the academic years, such as "Theological Literacy," "God in the City," "Church and the Future," "Faith and Citizenship," "Millennium Development Goals," "Themes in Religion and Science," "Religion, Peace and Political Engagement," and the nature of "Mission and Globalization." It is out of these contexts that these articles were chosen.

For many years institutionalized Christianity was grounded on convergences as well as divergences over doctrine, ethics and worship. With respect to ethical engagement, the apparently great achievement of the ecumenical work that followed 1910 is that it refocused the ethical debate from nuanced arguments to common interests. At the doctrinal level, it has managed to create a myriad of theologians who have revisited historical divergences, and started moving away from argumentative theology. With respect to worship, which is often seen to be the private sphere of religion, institutionalized Christianity displays the need for further conversation.

It is important to recognize some additional aspects of missional dialogue since 1910. First, there has been a movement away from the consciousness of a territorial religion, toward greater ethnographic consciousness, and finally, to the interiorization of the idea of a "missional church" in a post-colonial era. Secondly, some tension has developed between the consciousness of how we embody the hope for salvation that we profess with a sense of conveying this same hope to others in an instrumental fashion.

It is our hope that you will enjoy reading these stimulating reflections on world mission and Christianity. As editors we would like to express our gratitude to all our contributors for their service and commitment.

By Rodney L. Petersen & Marian Gh. Simion

# 1.
## What If God's Name is 01100100?

By Kwok Pui-lan
Episcopal Divinity School

When I was a doctoral student at Harvard, the library system was not yet computerized. Trying to find a book on Chinese art and mythology, one might need to check the card catalogues at Widener, Harvard-Yenching, and Tozzer libraries because they each had different classification systems. The Religion Index was not computerized and one had to comb through multi-volumes to find the information needed.

Whenever students asked me how did I survive the doctoral program, I simply answered: perseverance. I suffered through the process of computerization, but graduated before the debut of HOLLIS and the RI on CD-ROM. To my students' utter amazement, that was less than ten years ago. Today, they can go to the terminals of their school's library and find out if a book is available or has been checked out in the libraries of the BTI.

In The Road Ahead, Bill Gates argues that there were two major shifts in the history of communication: the introduction of movable type to Europe by Johann Gutenberg about 1450 and the advent of the information highway. Before Gutenberg, there were only about 30,000 books on the entire continent of Europe, nearly all Bibles or biblical commentary. In 1996, there were more than 2,360 million books sold in the US and books on religion comprised about 7.4 percent. There are thousands of websites on religion and spirituality, and YAHOO! locates 1457 websites related to "God."

Computer technologies have drastically changed our lives and many theologians have paid insufficient attention to this phenomenon, as Dr. Anne Foerst has argued in an article in the series on "Theological Literacy" in October, 1997. The information highway has revolutionized our ways of collecting, storing, retrieving, cross-referencing, and superlinking knowledge.

What constitutes theological literacy in the explosion of knowledge and who are the "authorities" to decide? Does one become more theologically literate by reading Augustine's City of God or by browsing the websites on feminist theology?

What is the point of spending hours trying to master the latest theological tome, when the current readership for serious theology is only about 13,000 people?

Comparable to the work of the monks in the Middle Ages who hand-copied manuscripts, corporations putting data into CD-ROMs are preserving knowledge for posterity. What kinds of religious data will be digitized and what will be left out? Will the digital medium be more user-friendly to people in the Third World than the print medium? The digital medium can preserve images, rituals, dances, and songs that can enlarge our theological imagination and repertoire. Is any school in the BTI teaching students how to interpret these diverse resources available on a CD? Will students hand in CDs as final projects in the near future? To prepare for "the road ahead," the study and the practice of "hermeneutics" in theological schools will have to be radically re-conceived and rapidly expanded.

Since connected online, I have been surfing in cyberspace, keeping in touch with the virtual theological community. I submitted an article to an editor in England, consulted a scholar in Jerusalem, collaborated with a feminist theologian in Japan, and monitored peace and justice issues in China through the amazing email. Since the 1970s, liberation theologians have argued for the contextualization of theology. Today, it is harder to define clearly where one's context begins and ends. The information highway has created the new poor who have no access to these computer technologies and who are Internet-challenged. Because of these new technologies, those of us living in metropolitan centers no longer have any excuse for not knowing what is going on in other parts of the world. The Other is not "out there." The other may be within the reach of our fingertips by simply typing http://www. the.other.com.

The computer technologies have changed the way we do research forever. Sometimes I still recall nostalgically the joy and triumph of finding a book after checking three card catalogues. Inculcating a little perseverance in theological students is not a bad idea either. But the most intriguing aspect of the information highway is its impact on how we think. In theological discourse, we have often relied on our analogical, symbolic, and metaphorical imagination. What will theology be like if God's name is rendered as

01100100, using the binary system in digitization? What will the attributes of God be in our digital imagination? Do we talk about attributes at all? What other categories will be needed? will we speak of God's omnipotence in terms of gigabytes, the Holy Spirit in terms of the web of fiber-optic cables, and salvation in terms of Super-antivirus?

Is somebody writing a book on 01100100 for the Dummies?

## 2.
## Learning from Other Religions
## as an Integral Part of Theological Education

By Francis X. Clooney, S.J.
Harvard Divinity School
*formerly faculty at* Boston College Department of Theology

Theologians and ministers of the Gospel in the 21st century must be well-informed about the beliefs and practices of people in the other faith traditions of the world, and must integrate this learning with their self-understanding as Christians. Practically, it is good policy to know our neighbors, and in the years to come we will increasingly be rubbing shoulders with people of other religions, right here in the United States. Intellectually too, interaction is inevitable; the very terms in which we present our faith—"faith," "revelation," "scripture," "God," "wisdom," "love,"—are alive in American culture and cannot be stipulated to have purely Christian eanings. Pastorally, many of the people with whom we work are already re-forming their spiritual and Christian identities in the context of pluralism, and we must learn from them if we are to speak to them. Spiritually, we ourselves must be willing to learn from other religious traditions if we wish to remain open to God; as Pope John Paul II has put it, "By dialogue we let God be present in our midst, for as we open ourselves to one another, we open ourselves to God." We need to learn from other religions in a way that is informed by the Christian Faith, that is in keeping with recognized methods of Christian theology, and yet that also eventuates in a transformed appropriation of Christian faith and spirituality.

These goals are large, but it is best to set modest expectations for ourselves and our students and to focus on practically feasible steps. We will never be able to learn all that needs to be known about even the "major" religions. We cannot finesse the question of content by an appeal to methodology, nor reduce interreligious learning to a general theory about religions. A course on "Christ and the world religions," for instance, will surely serve valuable purposes, but it will not inculcate the requisite skills for dealing from other traditions, any more than a course in hermeneutics might replace the actual study of Scripture. The best approach, I suggest, is to focus on particular examples. Students can learn a great deal by a case-study method, by select courses which open up new ways of thinking even if they do not cover a comprehensive range of data. I can imagine, for instance, courses such as "Family Ethics in Traditional China," "Images of God in Traditional African Cultures," "Islam in Contemporary America," and even more specific courses such as "Love of God in Vernacular Hinduism." The primary pedagogical value of a few well-presented examples should not be underestimated. A sophisticated course on one aspect of one religious tradition can uncover the concrete problems which invariably arise when we try to understand other religions without neglecting our own. Generalizations will have to be made on the basis of the cases, but these generalizations will pertain primarily to how we learn religiously and what we do with what we learn.

Very few schools have the resources to hire experts in various religious traditions, and most of the time faculty with other areas of expertise will be expected to teach the world religions courses if they are to be taught at all. Faculty may rightly be reluctant to teach outside their specialization, yet intelligent amateurism is viable if the new learning and new teaching are integrated with the professor's own established areas of expertise, content and methods. Courses such as those suggested in the previous paragraph could be tailored to the interests and capabilities of specific faculty, taught in one way by an exegete, another by a systematic theologian, and yet another by a historian or sociologist of religions. There is no good reason why inventive syntheses could not take place; a scripture scholar could introduce a comparative element into the New Testament introduction by taking a look at Rabbinic and Quranic methods of exegesis; a historian could highlight how missionary work in China affected the self-understanding of European Christians in the 17th and 18th centuries; and systematician could illuminate a Christian understanding of grace by examining how grace is explained in one or another school of Buddhism.

This new comparative literacy requires refined pedagogical skills, and these need to be developed and shared based on faculty experiences. The 1997-1999 consultation on "Teaching about World Religions in Theological

Schools and Theology Departments" at the Wabash Center, is a possible model for how faculty can work together in exploring the theological and pedagogical challenges related to teaching religions in a theological setting. A similar program could easily be undertaken in the BTI.

After the study of religions in their rich specificity has become a secure part of theological education, we will then be able to revisit disciplines such as the theology of religions and missiology, asking how knowledge of other religions affects our Christian self-understanding in these areas. For, there is no reason why a choice has to be made between informed empathy with other religious traditions and a renewed commitment to clear Christian identity. Comparative study clears our minds of useless and harmful preconceptions and helps us to confront more honestly the implications of preaching the Gospel in a world where the Good News is very much needed, but where we also have very much to learn from our non-Christian brothers and sisters. Indeed, keeping this balance is the whole point behind integrating the study of other religions into theological education.

# 3.
# *Ecumenism and Evangelicals*

By Kurt Anders Richardson
McMaster University
*formerly faculty at* Gordon-Conwell Theological Seminary

The relation of Evangelicalism to the ecumenical movement has been mixed. Since mid-century, Evangelicals have distanced themselves from their fundamentalist roots seeking to live their commitment to evangelism and biblical orthodoxy across denominational boundaries. Their kind of Christian identity was new: a lay oriented collaboration of Christians deeply indebted to the American democratic context that united loosely yet with great conviction for the freedom and propagation of the gospel of Jesus Christ.

As a child whose parents were touched by the ministry of Billy Graham in the early 1960's, there was always a sense in which denomination and trans-denominational ministry were presupposed. My own background is Baptist, but from the beginning of my Christian experience and personal faith there was a realization that faithful Christians—both ordained and non-ordained—were uniting for mission in unofficial but highly creative ways. Youth ministry down to the local level yet united by national Evangelical organizations affected me throughout my own childhood and had a vital role in my commitment to ministry at the age of 16. Now, 25 years later, working primarily in systematic theology and ethics but also pastorally, lessons I learned about Christian fellowship across denominational and confessional boundaries go way back to my earliest Evangelical context. In this short space I would like to make my comment along four lines: A focused diversity; new churches and alternative structures; new dialogue and new responsibilities; and the "household" of faith and the households of religion.

A focused diversity Ecumenically, American Evangelicalism could be described as a focused diversity of Christian believers. Overwhelmingly, the central concern that has united them and spawned thousands of organizations for national and international ministry has been the so-called "Great Commission" of the Gospel of Matthew: "Go into all the world and preach the gospel." In the last three decades, the carrying out of this mandate by Evangelicals has included a gradual diversification of their movement to include Catholic and Orthodox, mainline, "post-liberals" and "post-conservatives." Quite visible, however, is a kind of "congregational" ethos, that the lines of cooperation—always unofficial and usually informal—set the diverse parties free for creative accomplishment of the mission of the Church. There are, certainly, many weaknesses and mistakes, much room for maturation and learning; nevertheless, this ethos makes for responsiveness and modifiability of the basic fulfillment of the mandate so that it can be carried out more effectively, fruitfully and above all, irenically.

### New churches and alternative structures

The history of the official structures of international ecumenism does not include much representation from the stream of Evangelicalism. Indeed, in many contexts, both in this country and globally, there is still an attitude that runs: either Evangelicalism or Ecumenism. This is visible particularly in the parallel structures of the Lausanne/Manila Conferences put on through the global cooperation of Evangelicals in contrast to the assemblies of the WCC. By the end of the twentieth century, the emergence of very large Evangelical communities on all of the continents in some ways reinforces this trend. Alternative structures for mission, new denominations—indeed, whole new churches—are all about us and very possibly make any official international body hopelessly obsolete or unworkable.

### New dialogue and new responsibilities

Evangelicals are exhibiting new ecumenical initiatives even on the official side of the WCC and the historic churches. The eighties and nineties have seen a number of Evangelicals invited to assume significant leadership positions and to enter into very fruitful cooperative relationships. In many ways, this was automatic, given what amounts to their de facto majority status among Protestants in this country. On levels theological and ministerial, ecumenical encounter is becoming a way of life and work. This is perhaps most evident in the "Evangelicals and Catholics Together" documents produced in the last five years. Evangelicals have become hugely successful though their movements are particularly fragile—but where is late twentieth century Christianity not fragile?

### *The "household" of faith and the households of religion*

Evangelicals, to the extent that they truly develop a responsible ecumenism, will do so while maintaining their particular focus on the Great Commission of Christ. Evangelicals will want to protect a very biblically grounded sense of the term: oikumene. Ecumenism will be unalterably a global movement seeking and uniting the "household of faith." Based upon a "partnership in the gospel" rather than cultural privilege, Evangelicals will be seeking a commonality in Christian faith that is likely to only increase in diversity and richness. There is also a great deal of inter-religious dialogue going on, especially among the new churches as minority communities in non-Western contexts. But there like here, Evangelicals embody a real awareness of the differences among the households of the world religions. This last point brings up what is likely, the truly contentious issue among ecumenical theologians today: defining ecumenism. As one Evangelical theologian, I am committed passionately to the debate over what should be appropriate definitions of ecumenicity. In the meantime, there is an Evangelical ecumenism that is worth studying, understanding and embracing.

# 4.
## Interfaith, Ideology, and Ecumenism

By John Berthrong
Boston University School of Theology

There are always a host of reasons why ecumenism is important to the churches. We necessarily must remember the hope for reconciliation and visible unity that ecumenism expresses for Christians. Moreover, in a modern and religiously pluralistic world, interfaith relations and inter-Christian ecumenism are woven together in urgent and even appealing ways. The logic that demands Christian unity, though not uniformity, is the same that today generates a passionate commitment to interreligious dialogue on part of Christians around the world.

In fact, one of the insights that interfaith dialogue and interreligious cooperation contributes to the ecumenical conversation is a sharp awareness that unity in seeking important goals, such as the mending of creation in the face of the terrible ecocrisis, does not also mean a hegemonic uniformity of responses to the issues at hand. For instance, Thai Buddhist monks, inspired by the ecology movement in the West and informed by Liberation Theology from Latin America, have developed a unique way to defend the great remaining forests of their country. They ordain the trees as Buddhist monks because the trees are fellow living creatures. I am told that this wonderful idea has had some success. It is a perfect example of how religions can learn from each other, though no one expects the Thai monks to convert to the Christian faith any time soon.

There is yet another insight that has arisen from the interreligious response to the ecocrisis. There is a growing recognition that there is no single religious solution to the ecocrisis. It is a crisis so vast that it demands the attention of all thoughtful people, including religious and secular people around the globe. If Hindu colleagues in India provide us with new ways to viewing harmful consequences of building dams on (sacred) rivers, then it behooves Christians in North American to pay attention. As the late Carl Sagan argued, the ecocrisis is ultimately a spiritual crisis for the whole of humanity. If there were ever a truly "ecumenical" world crisis, the ecocrisis is it.

Work with what is sometimes called the "wider" ecumenism of interreligious relations prompts yet another set of reflections on inter-Christian ecumenical realities. Perhaps it is really more a confession. How many times have I heard people engaged in ecumenical conversations pause and say something like, "I find it easier to talk to fellow liberals (or conservatives) in dialogue across denominational boundaries than with members of my own church." The reason for this is that much of what divides the churches today is the liberal-conservative ideological split. Historical theological differences meant a great deal, but today the issues that threaten the unity of Protestant denominations aren't the grand theological ones anymore. The rending issues are the debates between conservatives and liberals.

Moreover, these ideological culture wars have effectively paralyzed the major Protestant denominations. If there is a liberal project, such interfaith dialogue, it will surely be contested and vetoed by the conservatives. If the conservatives want more mission and church growth, the liberals will try to block this aspect of church life. Just try to get a similar argument going on the doctrine of "total depravity" or double predestination. Even the clergy will hardly know what you are talking about if you conjure up some of the hoary theological issues of the Reformation and Counter Reformation. But raise the question of the ordination of women or homosexuals and the fires of debate spring up like some kind of Wagnerian operatic magic. I suspect that only the second coming of Jesus will break the ring of ideological fire that surrounds the bride of Christ these days.

With theological humor I sometimes suggest that we could use another interfaith insight to escape the present ideological problems of the Protestant churches. We could again follow the lead of our Jewish brothers and sisters. We should call an ecumenical "time out" and reorganize the churches into three new denominations, liberal or reformed, conservative, and orthodox. This would give the church bureaucracies something to do because they would have the task of figuring out where the prorated property, trust funds, and surplus bishops would go. The new churches could then act locally based on ideologically shared convictions and nationally on common pan-Christian goals. I dream of how vibrant such a reorganization would be. The Protestant churches could actually do something without the present bickering about liberal-conservative culture wars.

Alas, I have about as much hope for the ideological reformation of the churches of the historic reformation as I do for a quick and painless fix for the ecocrisis. However, I am sure that these are both issues that need the sustaining vision and hope that flows from the ecumenical movement and interfaith dialogue.

# 5.
# *Ecumenical Winter ... or Summer?*

By Gabriel Fackre
*formerly faculty at* Andover Newton Theological School


At a BTI anniversary some years ago, George Lindbeck spoke about the future of ecumenism. He was not very encouraging. Ventures in which he had participated were foundering and enthusiasm for others born of the ecumenically hopeful 1960s was waning. His advice? The best we can do right now is to pray for the pope and for Billy Graham."

Lindbeck's gloom became the conventional wisdom for many years, the forecast of an "ecumenical winter." Indeed, there has been plenty of evidence for just that in the weakening of conciliar Christianity and the emerging of a neo-tribalism in both theology and church life. But, strange to say, a *US News* and *World Report* story in July 1997 was captioned, "An Ecumenical Summer." Summer, not winter?

The report had to do with 1997 summer assembly votes involving North American Lutheran relations with other church bodies. The background of each was long-term dialogues based on substantial theological inquiry: an international Lutheran-Roman Catholic document on justification by faith proposing the lifting of mutual 16th century condemnations; an ELCA Lutheran-Episcopal Concordat and a Lutheran-Reformed Formula of Agreement on full communion" among the ELCA, the Presbyterian Church, USA, the Reformed Church in America and the United Church of Christ. I adduce the last two as evidence for my remarks here, and add to them a parallel venture, the nine-denomination "Churches in Covenant Communion: The Church of Christ Uniting" (COCU) due for defining decisions at its assembly this very month.

On the team of 12 theologians in the final four-year "Lutheran-Reformed Conversation" (along with BTI colleagues Ronald Thiemann and

Beth Nordbeck), I came to appreciate the kind of ecumenism which took doctrine with great seriousness, entailed structural consequences, and worked with honesty at both convergences and divergences. Previous teams had been at it for many decades. The vote to approve full communion (exchange of clergy, eucharistic hospitality, planning for joint mission) brought 45 years of theological soul-searching to a gratifying conclusion. In the concurrent dialogue, after approval by the Episcopal Church and a not quite two-third required majority vote by the ELCA assembly (six votes short), the Concordat has been revised by a joint working group led by Martin Marty and will be reconsidered this year and next by the two bodies. Prospects for a positive vote have been rated high. In the third development, eight of nine denominations have signed on to COCU, scaled back in 1984 from a more ambitious union plan to the present covenanting/full communion proposal. COCU has yet to receive Episcopal assent on the "reconciliation of ministries," but the possibilities of an alternative "recognition of ministries" are under consideration that would honor the degree of agreement already achieved and enable the nine Churches to go forward in some way, perhaps along the lines of advance being made in the Lutheran-Reformed agreement. Of special significance is COCU's model of catholicity in matters of race and ethnicity as it includes three major African-American denominations.

How are the foregoing not an ecumenical summer? Here are bilateral and multilateral conjunctions based on long-term theological dialogue and issuing in hard-won theological consensus. All conjoin ecumenical realism to ecumenical vision, disavowing sanguine expectations about union, but relentless in the pursuit of realizable unities. Each states or presupposes a tough-minded "mutual admonition," a formula developed in the Lutheran-Reformed conversation and cited by ecumenist Harding Myer as an important breakthrough. Admonition means a covenant to honor and learn from the others' unique gifts and to put forward one's own as a charism needed for the fullness of the Body. It joins a mutuality in affirmation of shared core doctrine. These dual mutualities may be the formula for surviving long ecumenical winters.

The Lutheran-Catholic proposal on justification is still in limbo because of a mixed response from the Vatican though approved by many Lutheran Churches. Nevertheless, it suggests at least spring if not a summer temperatures given the degree of amity and advance beyond previous polarization. And George Lindbeck, a key figure in that dialogue and barometer of ecumenical seasons? He has just been invited by the Minnesota Center for Catholic and

Evangelical Theology to draft a study document for a June consultation, "Ecumenism: Where Do We Go From Here?" Stay tuned.

The Harare assembly of the World Council of Churches points toward new and interesting directions for world ecumenism, ones noted in earlier columns: widening the arena of cooperation and conversation to include both marginalized constituencies and major Christian Churches heretofore neglected; more demanding efforts in interfaith outreach; a wide-ranging religious collegiality on issues of justice and peace. Attention to these important ecumenical horizons, however, must not obscure the less glamorous and often laborious history of bilateral and multilateral agreements. The theological community is a natural arena for encouraging such because this history takes with great seriousness the very tasks that theological schools are about. Why not the BTI as such a venue, as the church traditions involved in the bilateral and multilateral summer are represented in some of its schools and well-represented in its faculties? May a thousand such roses bloom in Boston.

# 6.
# *Ecumenism Matters*

By Liam C. Walsh, O.P.
University of Fribourg, Switzerland

Ecumenism matters because the Gospel matters. And the Gospel matters because it is the event, made known in word and ritual, that has radically changed the universe. The Gospel is a kind of "big bang" of God's grace, after which nothing was ever to be the same. It acts as a new explosion of creativity throughout the universe that, paradoxically, would hold everything together by the very energy that generates diversity. The Gospel is radically ecumenical: it is a power that makes divergent things come together—and hold together—in oneness.

The telling and celebration of this explosive event, and of its promise for our universe, is urgent. Jesus, in whom all saving energy was infinitely compressed so that it could burst forth and make all things new, sent those who had been with him from the beginning to preach and baptize. With their words and rituals, they were the bearers and the tellers of what the Spirit—in whose giving the Gospel event reached its fullness—was doing in the world. They were to spread the message to the ends of the known earth. They were to work in a time-span that might be measured in millennia, but that would surely come to an end when all things were recapitulated and brought to rest in Christ. They were to be missionaries, telling the world before it was too late where this expanding, diversifying and still unifying energy is coming from. The churches and the Church that they formed would be prototypes and agents of human—and indeed cosmic—unity in diversity. The Church, in embodying the Gospel as mission, is innately ecumenical.

If those who have been hearing and announcing the Gospel event as good news for two thousand years have not always succeeded in holding themselves together as they went their distinctive ways, the failure in unity has been more in the showing than in the being. It is Christ and the Spirit who bring and hold the world together in its journey towards this final recapitulation, and their energy never falters. The task of the churches is to how Christ and the Spirit are at work within the churches themselves, and to let that work happen and be seen happening in the world. Christians are to be the "showing forth," the sacrament of Christ and the Spirit. Christians have their failures in the showing. They have let their diversity isolate them and oppose one another. Their life has, too often for comfort, belied their words and their rites. Fortunately, the divine energy that the churches sacramentalize has always been there. The power that is at work in Christians—the power of Christ and of the Spirit—never ceases to be a force for unity. There, in this divine energy, is a divine ecumenism that precedes, is at the heart of, and is the fulfillment of Church ecumenism.

The unifying presence of Christ and the Spirit shows in the churches, in spite of their own failures. It shows in the range of Gospel gifts, of word and sacrament that are visible in each church. The churches proclaim the Gospel by proclaiming the word and celebrating the sacraments with which they themselves are gifted. But, if the gifts of any church are to be really a showing of the Gospel, of its power to hold the universe together, these must be made to take account of and do something about anything that separates this particular church from the others. Churches have to prize the oneness, holiness, catholicity and apostolicity that is manifested in their own communion. At the same time, they have to be wanting and working for the full oneness, holiness, catholicity and apostolicity that will let the world see who and what Christ really is, and let it feel the wonder of what the Spirit is doing in it.

This is the ecumenical imperative. It is not an option of church policy. It is what the Gospel, and the missionary proclamation of the Gospel, forces the churches to be and to do.

# 7.
## *Why Ecumenism Matters*

By Eduardo R. Cruz
Pontifical Catholic University of São Paulo, Brazil

Ecumenism did not matter that much in the first half of my life. Raised as a Roman Catholic in a largely Roman Catholic society, interaction with other religious groups was minimal. In those pre-Vatican II days, priests and nuns occasionally referred to other religions in a somewhat condescending tone. Tolerance, however, was the rule, and several of my friends and acquaintances were not Catholics. This status quo changed, at least at the level of consciousness, with my encounter with Liberation movements in Latin America and upon my entrance in a M.Div. program in the late seventies.

The real change from reason to the guts, however, had to wait my coming to Chicago, in order to pursue a doctoral degree in theology and science in the mid-eighties. First, because I chose a Lutheran school there for its academic credentials, and second because of a uniquely North American institution: the cluster of theological schools around renowned universities. That is the case with CCTS and BTI. In fact, there I had a palpable and challenging experience of religious otherness. The outcome was astonishing. Instead of seeing a kind of lukewarm soup of all religious traditions, or a threat to my own religious identity, I rather came to open my eyes to forgotten aspects of my Roman Catholicism, and value it all the more. The other helped me to find myself!

So the first answer to the question of the title is this: ecumenism matters because a true encounter with other religious traditions helps to enhance the understanding of our own, and therefore opens the possibility to strengthen our faith. But this answer is still too abstract. Besides being Roman Catholic, I am also Brazilian—part of the New World, one of the Americas, thrown in the midst of the tension between Anglo-Saxon and Latin America. When I first came to Chicago, Liberation Theology was at its height, and people there had a keen interest about the new possibilities open by a church coming from below. I do think that the Latin American experience brought to the life of North American churches some new awareness, but perhaps its importance has been overestimated.

Perhaps we were much too optimistic about movements for emancipation and "democracy" within and without the churches. In any case, today's situation has changed substantially. First because what is generally called "globalization" has been a mixed blessing, overemphasizing economy (widening the gap between the rich and poor in a worldwide level) in detriment of citizenship. Second because "fast-food" religion is on the rise (also in a worldwide scale), and not many people are willing to engage in the long-range effort of consciousness-raising and building grassroots communities. But, the seed was sown in good soil, even if we are not sure which species this seed belongs to.

How to make sure then that the tree, regardless of its final aspect, will grow to full maturity? There are certainly other people best qualified than I am to provide answers, so what follows is a very modest ending. My little experience has nonetheless shown that the dialogue between science and theology provides good ground for ecumenism, as well as further possibilities for the dialogue across the Americas. The basic laws of science and doctrines of theology, after all, are pretty universal in kind. Instead of bringing differences to the fore ("rich" north, "poor" south, or worse, "first world"—"third world"), we would better look for similarities, working together.

Fostering programs of exchange seems crucial to me—information, new developments, and especially people. NGOs (either church-related or not) are good vehicles for this purpose, adding experience and resources from each side. Recent programs of the Templeton Foundation, for instance, have brought visibility, continuity, professionalism and coherence to efforts to relate theology and science, and it has been the wise decision of this Foundation not to restrict these programs to the English-speaking world. Whatever the institutional milieu we find it fitting, it is my hope that economic, linguistic, and cultural barriers will not be an impediment for true ecumenism.

# 8.
# *The Deep Roots of Ecumenism*

By Grand Protopresbyter Georges Tsetsis
Ecumenical Patriarchate Permanent Representative to the WCC

In modern Church history, the first two decades of the twentieth century are considered as the dawn of a new promising period in Church relations. The repeated initiatives of the Ecumenical Patriarchate of Constantinople for reconciliation and cooperation (1902, 1904, 1920), the call of the World Missionary Conference of Edinburgh for a common Christian witness in the world (1910), the formation of the World Alliance for Promoting International Friendship Through the Churches (1914), as well as the Preparatory Conferences of the "Faith and Order" and "Life and Work" movements in process of formation (1920), marked a new beginning in Church relations and constituted praiseworthy attempts to abandon past practices and to lay the foundations of the ecumenical movement. This movement can be understood as an effort of Churches and many committed Christians to overcome past quarrels, to find new denominators for the Churches' witness and service to the world and thus to prepare the conditions to facilitate the restoration of their unity.

It should be stressed, however, that although the term "Ecumenical Movement" was used for the first time in the twenties in order to define the above development in interchurch relations, the idea of ecumenism per se is not a recent development in the life of the Church. On the contrary, it could be that ecumenism was at the very center of the Church's pastoral ministry, since apostolic times.

The liturgical praxis of the Church demonstrates most eloquently that ecumenism, in the sense of a mobilization for eliminating the scandal of division, has always been at the very center of the pastoral ministry of the One, Holy Catholic and Apostolic Church, since her establishment. It is not symptomatic that the eucharistic prayer of the Church in all ancient Liturgies, beginning with the one contained in the *Didache* (chapters IX and X) and ending with the Divine Liturgy of Saint John Chrysostom, includes essential elements such as the termination of schisms, the repression of heresies, the restoration of peace in the Church and the unity of the entire oikoumene in Jesus Christ.

Besides the liturgical practice of the Church, the conciliar history of the Church also speaks with equal eloquence about this very truth. Metropolitan Chrysostomos of Ephesus, referring to the way in which the Church had to deal with schisms and heresies, asks "What was the long and exhausting conciliar process? If not an effort to define the right faith and the right praxis of the Orthodox side, against the beliefs of the heterodox?" And he continues: "This process implied comparison of views, collegial discussion, dialogue and finally the crystallization of the doctrine, under the presence and breath of the Holy Spirit."

Ecumenism, both as a theological challenge and as an expression of the Church's willingness for Christian unity, has always been experienced in the Church. Begun during the first, fifth, eleventh and sixteenth centuries, it reemerged in the twentieth century when the Throne of Constantinople took its well-known initiative, calling upon the Churches to create a "League of Churches" (Koinonia ton Ekklision) in order to foster cooperation and promote unity. An initiative "without precedent in Church history," as Visser't Hooft once stated, it was favorably welcomed by many outstanding Anglican and Protestant church leaders who, confronted with their own chaotic separations, were also trying to unite their Churches and thus give to the world a common witness, in the framework of "Faith and Order" and "Life and Work."

And indeed the World Council of Churches was founded in 1948 after the merger of these two major components of the early ecumenical movement.

Ecumenical cooperation, however, goes much beyond the WCC or the National and Regional Councils of Churches.

A most significant ecumenical work is implemented today through a series of bilateral dialogues, with the clear intention to create mutual understanding between the Churches, to remove progressively past condemnations and achieve visible unity in one faith and in full sacramental communion.

These dialogues are conducted with a varying degree of success, according to the circumstances and to their historical context. They express the determination of those engaged in them to facilitate a better understanding between the Churches and denominations and prepare the way towards Christian unity.

It is worth noting that these dialogues, by focusing on controversial doctrinal issues, which divided the Churches for centuries, were able to reach remarkable theological agreements and convergence.

The question is whether these agreements can be meaningful for the people of God or be relevant in the context of the day to day life and witness of a parish.

The late Dr. Visser't Hooft once remarked that "There is a very real danger in the bilateral dialogues of becoming esoteric, for they are speaking in a language and formulas which are only really understood by those who are participating and not by the average Church members."

Indeed an academic dialogue, based on positions, texts and arguments, a dialogue which overlooks—or even ignores—the pastoral problems of the Churches in a given context, is condemned to remain a theoretical exercise, with little impact in the effort to restore Christian unity and with no influence in the life of our believers.

This is why pastoral, social and ethical problems can no longer be excluded from the bilateral dialogues. Analogous to the connection between doctrine and worship is the inseparable connection between orthodoxia and orthopraxia. An orthopraxia makes ethics, no less than dogmatics, an indispensable element of any interchurch dialogue. Church doctrine, spirituality and action are so intimately related, that they are all integral parts of today's ecumenical dialogue.

# 9.
# *The Ecumenical Nature of Hymnody*

By Carl P. Daw, Jr.,
The Hymn Society in the United States and Canada
Boston University School of Theology

*"...we are all singing each other's hymns*
*and are being nourished by that experience."*

One of the most effective illustrations I know of the ecumenical dimensions of hymnody in these closing years of the twentieth century occurred in the preparation of the 1992 Hymnal: A Worship Book, jointly prepared by the Church of the Brethren and representatives of two Mennonite denominations. One of the challenges they faced was that heretofore there had been a customary first hymn in Brethren hymnals and a (different) customary first hymn in Mennonite hymnals. There was no way both "first hymn" traditions could be perpetuated: 1A and 1B simply would not work. So they very creatively set out to identify an opening hymn that would give voice to their common understanding of worship. As it turned out, the first hymn in this joint North American Brethren-Mennonite hymnal is written by a Dutch Roman Catholic!

Despite all the juridical and doctrinal impediments that separate churches in other matters, it is immensely encouraging to see how congregational song operates as a force for Christian unity. In part, the emergence of a significant body of shared hymnody has been the natural result of many years—even centuries—of use in a variety of worship styles: the hymns that have endured tend to be used in more churches.

But this convergence in the hymnic repertoire has not occurred entirely by happenstance. In 1968 the Consultation on Ecumenical Hymnody (CEH) was formed by representatives of eleven Protestant churches and the

Roman Catholic Church, and they produced in 1971 a list of 150 hymns identifiable as the common core of Christian hymnody. Because several hymnals were published following the compilation of this original list, a revised list containing 227 hymns was agreed on in late 1976. This full list of texts and tunes was printed in the October 1977 issue of THE HYMN, the quarterly journal of the Hymn Society of America (as it was then known). The timing of this consultation and publication was most propitious and influential, because nearly every major denomination in North America has produced a new hymnal (and often a subsequent hymnal supplement) in the twenty-plus years that have followed. It is significant that a number of these books provide in an index some explicit indication of the hymns included from this CEH list, while others implicitly reflect this growing consensus by their selections.

The work of identifying a common hymnic repertoire has continued. At the request of The Hymn Society in the United States and Canada, Dr. C. Michael Hawn of the Perkins School of Theology at Southern Methodist University undertook a survey of forty hymnals published in Canada and the United States from 1976 to 1996. His study yielded a list of 314 hymns which appear in at least ten hymnals (i.e. in at least 25% of the volumes examined) and was published in the July 1997 issue of THE HYMN. Of this number, a little more than half (167) had appeared on the 1977 CEH list, but there are also a significant number of hymns (44) written since 1950. Looking to the future, Dr. Hawn appends a list of 140 post-1950 hymns which did not occur frequently enough to be included in his primary list but which seem to be gaining ecumenical use. This "Provisional List of Ecumenical Hymnody" identifies hymns appearing in at least three hymnals published since 1976.

When it is recognized that an average hymnal contains only about 600 hymns, it is really quite encouraging to consider how much convergence is represented by these growing lists of ecumenical hymnody. Editorial committees for these books are nearly always aware of the work that has been done to identify this common treasury of hymns and customarily begin their work by selecting texts and tunes from this repertoire, rounding it out with selections reflecting the particular theological understandings and liturgical patterns of its intended users.

It is also noteworthy that denominational origin is no longer an essential criterion either for inclusion or exclusion. As the opening example of the Dutch Roman Catholic hymn beginning the Brethren-Mennonite hymnal demonstrates, we are all singing each other's hymns and are being nourished by that experience. When a composer phoned our office recently to ask for a list of text writers in his particular tradition, I could name a few; but I also had to tell him that denominational allegiance rarely figures in the use of hymns these days. A further example of this welcome trend is the frequency with which denominational hymnals are being issued in an ecumenical version as well as a denominational one. All that really changes is the packaging: the same collection is simply sold with another name and/or a different cover. Even the marketing people have recognized that hymnody is now an ecumenical matter!

Like the development of a common lectionary that fosters the reading of the same scripture passages week by week in many different churches, the emergence of a shared body of hymnody further strengthens the awareness of an underlying unity sometimes obscured by our separate traditions.

Though we sing in varied voices, we are all singing God's song.

# 10.
## *Principles of Healing in Rwanda*

By Rhiannon Lloyd, MD
Reconciliation Networks of Our World

This article is extracted from a paper delivered by the Welsh psychiatrist Dr. Rhiannon Lloyd at the recent conference of Reconciliation Networks of Our World. It is used by permission. It is a part of a series of reflections on the conference as we work at what it means to be agents of reconciliation in our settings. During the past few years, it has been both a challenge and a privilege to visit Rwanda on numerous occasions, conducting seminars at the request of local Christian leaders on Healing, Forgiveness and Reconciliation. Here are some of the principles involved.

### *1) Recognizing the Church as*
### *God's Agent of Healing and Reconciliation*
In every situation, God is the God of hope, (Ro 15:13), and He places His hope in His people. Eph 3:10 - In every nation, His strategy is to use the church. Col 1:27 - The hope of glory for any nation is Christ within His people in that nation. Jesus said we are the light of the world! (Mat 5:14-16; Php 2:14-16) We are to shine like lights in the darkness because we are different, and what makes us different is that we think differently! Our lives have been transformed by the renewing of our minds. (Ro 12:1-2; Php 2:5; Eph 4:22-24) We are not conformed to the surrounding society. In Rwanda, the church failed to speak out and oppose the terrible injustices, and so became part of the problem. But God still believes in His church! After the resurrection, Jesus returned to a defeated group of disciples that were full of fear and had lost their vision. Yet, Jesus believed in them! When He appeared behind the locked doors, He said, "Peace be with you! As the Father sent me, so send I you."

God wanted to speak new hope into His church in Rwanda, especially to His faithful followers who had not betrayed their Lord, but who had persevered in the face of incredible suffering. They were now to be His agents of healing. But first they needed to be healed themselves. That's why we began with the strategy of calling together Christian leaders from every denomination and ethnic group to spend three days together in God's presence where they could encounter His healing love.

### *2) Finding the Right Sequence for the Seminar*

I believe that understanding and experiencing God's heart is the foundation of all healing, and so we had to begin there. From there, we could move on to find healing through the Cross for our inner wounds. By reading Isaiah 61 at the start of His ministry, Jesus made it clear that this was a priority for Him. It is very difficult to forgive while the heart is full of pain, but once we begin to experience healing, our hearts are free to forgive, and then to begin to think about reconciliation. To talk about forgiveness and reconciliation before discussing and experiencing healing is similar to trying to put a roof on a house before building the walls.

### *3) Overcoming Cultural Barriers In Expressing Emotion*

Having taken similar seminars in Liberia I was surprised to find that the culture of Rwanda regarding handling grief was very different from that of West Africa. Whereas in Liberia people express their emotions very freely, in Rwandese culture there is little expression of emotion, and no word for emotion in their language! Shedding tears is seen as a sign of weakness, and from an early age they are taught to always appear strong. For men especially, public expression of grief is unacceptable. They have a saying that a man's tears should flow into his stomach. They also believe that talking about traumatic experiences traumatises them even more. This was obviously a major obstacle to helping people towards healing! I wondered how to overcome this without in any way implying that my culture was superior. I found that the only acceptable way (as well as using medical evidence) was to focus on Jesus as the transcultural model of perfect humanity from whom all cultures could learn. Starting from this foundation we were then able to have lively discussions examining our self-protective coping mechanism, and this resulted in taking steps towards giving each other permission to feel.

### 4) Finding God in the Midst of Suffering

I usually began my seminars by asking the questions that were agitating in most people's hearts. "Where was God in April 94? Did He send these troubles? Has God abandoned us?" I wanted to create a safe place where participants could own their doubts and voice their inner questions without fear of being condemned. Story telling is a well-received form of teaching in Rwanda, and so I often made use of personal testimony, telling them of my struggles and my own pilgrimage to find a God of love in the midst of my family's sufferings. We tried to grapple honestly with the problem of human suffering, looking at the devastating consequences of the fall, the will of God vs. man's freedom of choice etc. I encouraged them as church leaders to allow people to ask their questions, and to be merciful with those who doubt, seeking a deeper understanding of God's ways and a new revelation of His heart. We focused on God's pain when His will is not done on earth, (Gen 6:5-6; Luke 13:34; 19:41-44) and how He suffers with us. (Isa 63:9)

### 5) Discovering Jesus as the Pain Bearer

It's only when we are reassured of God's intentions and feelings towards us that we can risk coming to Him with our pain. Something that has transformed my own life and my counselling is discovering Jesus as Pain Bearer as well as Sin Bearer. Isaiah 53:4 tells us that He bore our griefs and sorrows. It's not only our sins which are on the Cross, but all the consequences of sin. The whole tragic human condition is there. The Cross deals with our woundedness as well as our sinfulness. In our seminars, we looked at the Lamb who is inviting us to offload our grief onto Him, saying "Let Me do the hurting instead of you". They were able to grasp this concept, and here I witnessed pain being expressed, often in loud wails, as they brought their sorrow to Him. We would do this as a group experience, as individual counselling is not culturally understood, or even feasible given the scale of the trauma. The whole community is traumatised! To make the transfer of pain to Jesus more real, we used the symbolism of nailing their terrible stories to a large wooden cross which we transported around Rwanda. We would then take the cross outside and burn the papers. Afterwards I heard many encouraging testimonies. e.g. "I've been to many seminars, but this was different because I was able to leave my pain at the cross. My heart is so healed!- everyone in Rwanda needs to do this!

### 6) The Need to Hear and be Heard

Before pouring out their pain to the Lord, they also needed to listen to each other's hearts. We put people from different ethnic groups, and different denominations, into small groups together, and asked them to share together their stories. They were not only to listen to the facts but to listen to the pain in each other's hearts. Often there was resistance to doing this, but in the end the vast majority agreed, and we found that the dividing walls began to be demolished at this point. This willingness to listen to each other with compassion was especially important after the refugees returned to Rwanda from the camps in Zaire and Tanzania, when there was much fear, suspicion and hostility in the country.

### 7) Understanding Real Forgiveness

We talked about the transfer of pain to Jesus as being a prerequisite to being able to forgive from the heart, as Scripture requires of us. All too often I heard people say "I've forgiven - it's all past" as a means of avoiding facing the pain. Others opposed the church preaching forgiveness, thinking it meant condoning the wrong that had been committed. We needed to understand Biblical forgiveness, and its cost. I believe that our forgiving others requires the atoning sacrifice of the Lamb just as much as our receiving God's forgiveness. There's got to be Someone who can carry the sin sinned against us, bear our pain for us and take responsibility for ministering to our wounded hearts before we can truly forgive. It was only on the third day, after bringing their pain to the cross, that we would begin to teach on forgiveness, only to discover that a miracle had already taken place in the hearts of many the previous afternoon. So many testified of having left their hatred behind at the Cross and now being ready to forgive. But what if there is no evidence of repentance on the part of the offender? Can there be forgiveness then? I believe the key is found in 1 Peter 2:23. Jesus could forgive the unrepentant by committing his case into the hands of a Just Judge. There will be a day of judgment, and the unrepentant will be judged, but those who repent will find mercy. We can safely entrust our case into the hands of this Judge, and refuse to be the judge ourselves. Our hearts will then be set free.

### 8) Discovering Jesus as Redeemer

Another key was to discover Jesus as the Redeemer, - not only of our sins but of all our lives` tragedies. As we discover and experience His heart in the place of our greatest darkness, He can then 'turn our trials into gold' as in Keith Green's song. Instead of working against us, God can even make these worst tragedies work for us, so that we can continue living having been enriched within. Holding on to the bigger picture of God being able to redeem everything gives us hope to face the future. Identifying the good things that had resulted from the suffering, and the Light that shone in the darkness was always a cause for much rejoicing. Jn 1:5 tells us that "the light shines in the darkness but the darkness could not comprehend it. A better translation says, "the darkness could not overpower it," and it never will! Jesus always has the last word!

### 9) Exploring God's way of Dealing with Ethnic Conflict
We spent quite a lot of time looking at the roots of ethnic conflict, and where we learn our beliefs and prejudices. Because our ethnicity gives us a significant part of our identity, ethnic conflict is an attack on the core of our being. Here again I used my own testimony of growing up feeling like a second class citizen because I was Welsh. We focused on two ways of coming to a place of reconciliation: First, we needed to discover our identity as citizen's of God's community as with God's call to Abraham to leave his natural ethnic background. Second, I shared with them how God had disarmed my heart of resentment and prejudice against the English through the repentance of some English Christians on behalf of their forefathers. I have found that identificational repentance is a very powerful key to healing woundedness. (i.e. taking on the priestly role of repenting on behalf of our nation, people-group, forefathers, men, women, fathers, mothers, doctors etc. etc. It cannot absolve the guilt of the past, but it can release grace in the present for the offended to be able to forgive.) Each time I taught on this, God said to me "You start!" And time after time, God gave me a gift of repentance as a white European in Africa. I confessed the sins of our forefathers, asked for their forgiveness, and prayed for the healing of the African people. This often became the catalyst for heart change in them, opening up a whole new dimension in working towards reconciliation. Though it was completely uncultural for them, both Hutu and Tutsi began to stand in the gap, asking forgiveness on behalf of their people group as well as confessing their own sinful attitudes. In seminar after seminar we saw them weeping in each other's arms as God did a deep reconciling work amongst us. God anointed a song by David Ruis, "We will break dividing walls" which someone translated into Kinyarwanda, as a further means of touching hearts deeply. They love singing, so music was often a powerful communicator.

## 11.
## The First Globalization?
## The Internationalization of the Protestant
## Missionary Movement Between the World Wars

By Dana L. Robert
Boston University School of Theology

The global vision intrinsic to Christianity–that of one world, one Kingdom of God under Jesus Christ–has been both the motive and purpose behind much missionary fervor. Yet, the mission of the church has been conducted within rather than above human history: Protestant missions emerged in the context of the Enlightenment, the industrial revolution, and the subsequent expansion of capitalism and modernization. With its internal logic of universalism, or catholicity (Robert Schreiter suggests that catholicity is "the theological equivalent of globalization." See Richard Bliese, "Globalization," in *Dictionary of Mission. Theology, History, Perspectives,* eds. K. Muller, T Sundermeier, S. Bevans, R. Bliese (Maryknoll: Orbis, 1998), 176), Christian mission of necessity finds itself in dialogue with the secular globalizing tendency of the historical moment—whether that be European expansionism, western capitalism, or the world wide web. (While mission scholars would not equate Christian missions with globalization itself, there is a theoretical and practical problem of how to relate to secular globalization, how to influence it, and how to avoid being so closely identified with it that when globalization's time has passed, the mission of the church does not get washed away with the ebbing tide of popular support.)

The Anglo-American, Protestant missionary movement of the 1920s and 1930s functioned within the globalizing discourse of "internationalism"— a moral vision of one world that emerged after the horrors of World War I, and stemmed from the idealism of Woodrow Wilson's Fourteen Points. Internationalism launched a massive pacifist movement, brought into being the League of Nations and the World Court, and established the idea of the rights of self-determination for all peoples. (For a discussion of the internationalist movement in the United States, and its opposition to isolationism, see William Kuehl and Lynne K. Dunn, *Keeping the Covenant: American Internationalists and the League of Nations, 1920-1939* (Kent, Ohio: Kent State University Press, 1997). On the pacifist aspect of internationalism, see Charles Chatfield, *For Peace and Justice: Pacifism in America, 1914-1941* (Knoxville: University of Tennessee Press, 1971). Not only did sectors of the missionary movement embrace internationalism, but to a far greater extent than with the current business and technology-oriented definitions of globalization, the missionary movement helped to shape it, participated in it, and both defended and critiqued it at a grassroots level. In their most optimistic phase during the 1920s, mission advocates were accused of confusing internationalism with the Kingdom of God. Particularly in North American mainline churches, it became hard to distinguish internationalism from the mission impulse itself.

While internationalism was central to mainline Protestant missions in the 1920s and 1930s, recent scholarship has not used it as an interpretive framework for the missionary issues of the era. It has preferred to interpret the interwar period in light of the Kraemer/Hocking debate, or the tension between evangelistic and social gospel approaches to missions. My interest is to explore the relationship between internationalism and indigenization in the mission movement between the world wars, with primary reference to a North American conversation. In the course of my on-going work I hope to demonstrate that internationalism and indigenization were two sides of the same coin.

The globalizing vision of one world stood in tension with the cultural particularities that emerged in relationship to the global context itself. Internationalism demonstrated all the complexity that bedevils globalization in the early twenty-first century—a shifting set of both secular and religious definitions, and assumptions of universality both challenged and affirmed by nationalistic or particular ethnic identities. In possible continuing reflections here, I will draw upon my research to place the mission thought of the 1920s and 1930s in the larger context of internationalism, and then explore briefly the parallels with globalization today.

## 12.
## *A Global Awakening for National Policy: Social Policy after September 11*

By Thomas Massaro, S.J.
Boston College School of Theology and Ministry

I suspect that many Americans are, like me, torn between two conflicting desires. On one hand, we yearn for nothing more than the opportunity to revert to our comfortable pre-September eleventh ways, even if some aspects of our culture and routines now seem a bit frivolous. On the other hand, we feel the steady pull of conscience, to move beyond business as usual and meet the recent challenges to our nation by reforming our ways. In our more articulate moments, we might even dare to speak about somehow proving our worthiness of the blessings of freedom and prosperity we have so long enjoyed and taken for granted. It may be going too far to say that we expect a rebirth of our nation, but if there is any truth to the axiom that "nothing will ever be the same again after September eleventh," then it is fair game to offer suggestions for constructive change.

Social policy is one of the areas upon which the terrorist attacks cast new light. It is my fervent hope that our nation will seize this historic opportunity to demonstrate a renewed national commitment to combat poverty, that "crisis in slow motion." America's "war on poverty" is at best a dormant and neglected struggle. Even the phrase sounds anachronistic, a quaint reminder of heady days of some previous era, but surely nothing relevant to the new millennium. In any case, conventional wisdom runs, the timing is wrong. We need to devote our full attention to the war on terrorism. There is nothing left over for a mundane problem like poverty. Three responses to this argument follow.

First, there is ample historical evidence that external threats to a nation's security may serve as catalysts for more generous social welfare policies. At the end of the Second World War, our ally Britain discovered within itself the resolve to adopt revolutionary policies to combat poverty. The wartime solidarity that prevailed amidst the horrors of the Blitz and the bloody campaigns of the war was honored and amplified in universal policies to provide income security to all citizens, since members of all social classes had risked and lost their lives for that nation. The explosion of welfare guarantees a system of national health care, unemployment benefits and sharply expanded public housing marked a definitive break from the previous classbound system that sharply divided and stratified British society. Eligibility was universal because wartime sacrifices had been endured by all. The postwar British government would allow no Brit to starve. The lesson for America is not necessarily to imitate the often-maligned British welfare system, but rather to cultivate our sense of civic belonging and to convert our surge of patriotism into tangible measures to combat preventable poverty in our midst and assist all needy Americans.

Second, we are overdue for a revival of antipoverty measures. Such efforts have tended to follow thirty-year cycles. The twentieth century witnessed peaks of concern about poverty around 1905 (at the height of the Progressive Era), 1935 (the landmark Social Security Act was passed in the midst of the Great Depression) and 1965 (the legislative climax of Johnson's Great Society). The expected revival of social concern regarding poverty in the mid-nineties was short-circuited by the ascendancy of Newt Gingrich and his Contract with America. If legislative victories are to be won in the coming years (for example, in next year's reauthorization of the 1996 welfare reform law), they may perhaps be interpreted as a long delayed denouement of this turn of the wheel. Conversely, new anti-poverty measures may be viewed as vindication of the axiom that "war rushes history," as our patriotism may convert the scourge of poverty from a mere background condition we tolerate to a front burner problem demanding immediate attention. If the "war on terrorism" proves to be precisely what it takes to revive the war on poverty, we may find ourselves looking back to the inspiration of Franklin Roosevelt, whose Four Freedoms formulation explicitly linked "Freedom from Fear" and "Freedom from Want."

Third, the most encouraging news I have detected in the aftermath of the terrorist attacks regards attitudes toward federal power. There seems to be a merciful moratorium in the usual clamoring to "get government off our backs." For the first time in decades, government is widely portrayed not as the problem but as the solution, or at least as part of the solution to our extraordinary challenges. While by no means abrogating the principle of subsidiarity and the proper role of the non-public and non-profit sectors, the events of September eleventh have reminded us of the built-in limits of private sector efforts to combat complex social problems. It has been sobering to many observers to realize that most of the heroes of this new era, including firemen, rescue workers, air marshals, soldiers and elected officials, are public employees. Crises make strange bedfellows indeed, as proposals for unprecedented government activism and huge commitments of resources to combat terrorism are coming from unusual quarters. If advocates for low income Americans can make a persuasive case for the link between homeland security and income security, we may witness a long-overdue revival of the war on poverty.

Prominent among these advocates are religious voices. Most impressive is Call to Renewal, a Christian anti-poverty alliance of evangelicals, liberal Protestants and Catholics of many ethnic backgrounds led by Jim Wallis. Potential partners in a coalition of conscience are numerous, both secular and religious in character. Broad coalitions tend to use diffuse languages in this case, of common good, social responsibility, human rights, stewardship and preferential option for the poor. Efforts to revive the anti-poverty energies of our nation should emphasize public-private partnerships, new commitments to job training, education, tax advantages and emergency assistance to poor families. However we speak of our concerns or whatever strategies we encourage, advocates of renewed national efforts against poverty will do well to emphasize the linkage between our nation's twin desires: to secure our freedom and to use it wisely. Perhaps the terrorist attacks have shocked us out of our complacency regarding threats not only to peace, but to social justice as well.

# 13.
## Theological Literacy: A First Globalization

By Rodney L. Petersen
Boston Theological Institute

W*hat do we mean when we say God*? This is a question asked by former priest and Haitian President Jean-Bertrand Aristide. It has a different resonance for one growing up in *Cite Soleil*, Port-au-Prince's largest slum from one living in Palm Beach, Florida, U.S.A. But if "God" means "God" then the term has the same referent whether one is impoverished or wealthy. In this light theologian John H. Yoder writes, "The world of the twenty-first century will not be able to back away from having become one world."

Theology is the conscience of the Church in this one world. It deals with the "real thing" whatever our social status, race, or gender might be. It is a tool for learning and an instrument of understanding, not the merit badge of the privileged and learned. Everyone can become theologically literate in some sense because everyone is a theologian as they try to find their place in the world and make sense of it. Catholic and ecumenical in scope, evangelical and pastoral in intent, theology is shaped not only by scripture and church tradition but also by the levels of human organization and technological assumption that shape our experiences and ways of reasoning.

Much is hidden under the language of theology as philosophers of suspicion have taught us – much that makes the one world less than what it truly is. This diminishes us. Theology becomes ideology when the mystery of its referent is lost or our hope is invested in that which is less than ultimately real. Two tendencies in theology have been to orient theological thinking either in relation to a vertical and transcendent or horizontal and immanent dimension. Particular social concerns can often become flash points for division, as happened before the Fifth Assembly of the World Council of Churches at Nairobi, and happens today. Theological literacy is, in the first place, learning to give a reason for the hope that is in us (I Peter 3:15). It can mean more than this. It can also mean learning to think theologically which implies a more self-conscious effort at theological reasoning against a global horizon. The Apostle Paul offers an example of this in his letter to the Corinthians when he offers warnings from Israel's history as applicable to disciples of Jesus (I Cor. 10) or in his letter to the Galatians suggesting rules for interpretation of scripture (Gal. 4:21-31). In both cases, whether immediate or self-conscious, theological literacy is learning to discern and discuss what is the real thing.

Theological reflection on what is really most important in life happens through language. This is one reason why theological studies have often emphasized the importance of learning languages, the languages of the Bible and the languages of contemporary societies. Augustine is one of the first Christian theologians to stress the value of language. Especially helpful in this regard are his works On the Teacher (A. D. 389) and On the Trinity (A. D. 399-419), as well as On Christian Doctrine (A. D. 396). Each was written during a different period of his life. The general conclusion Augustine reaches in On the Teacher is that while human teachers teach us the meaning of words or signs, Christ, dwelling in the mind, can take us to the spiritual truth intended. In doxological fashion, Augustine writes that Christ is the source both the objects encountered and the light that illuminates them for our understanding.

Later in life, with the responsibility of a community dependent upon him, Augustine takes up the question of what can be known through language, or signs, once again. In On Christian Doctrine, they are said to carry us to divine things. Writing about the language of the Bible, signs and what they signify, he continues from where he left off in *On the Teacher*, Augustine stresses the triadic nature of signification: there is the object for which the sign stands, the sign itself, and the interpreter. The need for interpretation as an aid to theological literacy has spawned schools through the church's history. One might say that what one cannot agree on in worship is taken up for debate in newly founded schools with many of the modern universities even of our era dating to the first Scholasticism of the twelfth century.

Interpretation implies the need for a theology of personhood inclusive of all persons, a self-understanding of the ones involved in interpretation. Contemporary research in artificial intelligence has challenged the concepts of human dignity, the formation of the self, and identity or personhood as evolved in the tradition. However, the work of John D. Zizioulas, and others, has helped to sharpen our appreciation of the tradition through the retrieval of an Orthodox, or early Byzantine, understanding. This parallels Karol Wojtyla's (John Paul II) ontological neo-Thomism, grounding personhood in existential metaphysics, with a phenomenological description of "person" in terms of conscious acts through which one experiences substantial subjectivity. Early Christian theology was forced to derive a new metaphor for Being with anthropological implications for human self-understanding because of the cosmological revolution of which it was a part. As with Judaism, early Christian theology was drawn to conceive of God, not the world, as being absolute. The biblical doctrine of *creatio ex nihilo* obliged theology to trace ontology back to God, not the world, grounding the person as with Thomas not in necessity as a product of nature or even nurture, but in a form of freedom derivative of divinity.

Theological literacy, a first globalization, asks persons as interpreters to uncover what is finally real and live in its light. In relation to metaphysics, this has often been to ground theology in the energies or will of God while acknowledging the greater mystery of Being. In relation to logic, this has meant a line of argument or search for what is substantial and enduring. In relation to politics, this has meant accommodation to human needs and cultural patterns. Each of these three domain, ontology, epistemology, and ethics call us to a realism of presentation whereby they are one with the presumed content. Each reflects not only a search for certitude but also a desire for authenticity.

This search for what is real lies at the heart of theological anthropology, "You have made us for yourself, Lord, and our heart is restless until it rests in you" (Augustine). Commenting, John Paul II writes: "In this creative restlessness, beats and pulsates what is most deeply human – search for truth, the insatiable need for the good, hunger for freedom, nostalgia for the beautiful and the voice of conscience." Good theology, reflective of theological literacy, brings this search close to us, makes it palpable and vivid, through narrative and story.

## 14.
## Global Mission as Scholarship
## and the Demographic Transformation of the Church

By Andrew Walls
*formerly faculty at* Princeton Theological Seminary
*professor emeritus at* University of Edinburgh

Christian scholarship follows Christian mission and derives from Christian mission. The demand for scholarship occurred as soon as the Gospel crossed its first cultural frontier. In particular, once the word about Jesus Christ was translated into Greek, and entered into a Greek thought world without the built-in controls natural to Greek speaking Jews, all sorts of new questions (for instance about the proper way to express the relationship between the divine savior and the One God) were raised that were not likely to be aired when all the believers in Jesus were Jews. As the Christian mission to the Greek world expanded, Christian theology expanded too. Christians made discoveries about Christ that were only possible when their deepest convictions about him were expressed in Greek, and pondered using Greek indigenous categories and styles of debate. Why should they take notice of a story about a Jewish carpenter? Distortions, exaggerations, misunderstandings about Christianity abounded. Christianity, after all, was but one of a range of religious options on the market, packaged as schools of philosophy or schemes for understanding the cosmos.

We can chart the development of scholarly activity through those early centuries of evangelization that preceded and made possible the debates of the age of the great councils. Three figures may stand as representative of different stages in that development. First there is Paul, a learned and culturally sensitive Jewish missionary, who delved as deeply into Hellenistic culture as perhaps any outsider. He could take Hellenistic words and ideas like *mysterion* and *pleroma* and flood them with Christian meaning, and daringly use them to re-interpret Christ in Hellenistic terms. The second figure is Justin, the converted philosopher, who having investigated all the philosophical schools eventually chose to teach Christianity as the true philosophy. The third representative figure is Origen, child of Christian parents, brought up on the Scriptures but thoroughly educated in Greek learning too. Origen's scholarly achievement is immense. Not only did he invent, or give new impetus to, new areas of scholarship – textual criticism, systematic theology, the Biblical commentary - he brought almost every trend of existing philosophy and science into Christian service. As a teacher, this activity was not sustained in a setting of academic calm, but one of uncertainty and insecurity.

For all its antiquity and confidence, all was not well with the Greek cultural heritage in those centuries when Christianity was making its way in the Hellenistic world. Paul on the Areopagus in Athens is respectful, if gently ironic, when he addresses the philosophers there; his companion Luke, however, notes their lack of high seriousness. The only thing they wanted, he says, was novelty. In the century, the young Justin, seeking the vision of God that Plato had posed as the goal of the philosophic life, was shocked to find how anxious professional philosophers could be to settle the tuition fees. Philosophy, once a moral and religious discipline, a search for liberating truth, was becoming a profession, a job, a career. It was getting tired and given to recycling ideas. Its last real flourish was with Origen among the Christians and with his contemporary Plotinus among their opponents; but for all the latter's vigor and wealth of ideas, the resources of the Greek tradition were wearing thin. It was the Christians who renewed them, and by that means saved the Greek Academy and prolonged its life. It was Christianity, a teaching that had at first appeared utterly irreconcilable with Greek culture, that helped to preserve it, giving new life to some of its vital and authentic elements.

It would not be hard to point to other instances of scholarship arising out of mission. We could look eastwards from the Roman Empire where the battle for the Greek intellectual heritage was won, and observe Syriac speaking Christians spreading the Gospel through Mesopotamia and Iran and across Central Asia until in 635 AD (much the same time as the King of Northumbria in northern England was hearing it) it came to the Emperor of China. That long missionary trail across the largest continent is also a trail of libraries. Wherever the Christians went they took books, and the encounter with new cultures, as the Chinese evidence makes clear, caused them to translate books and to write new ones. The Chinese emperor of the day was himself a scholar, who spent half of each day in study. His first concern was to see what books the Christians had brought with them, and to get them translated, and to review them himself. It was on this basis that Christianity was permitted to spread in his empire. The surviving documents show these Christians trying to present Christianity in Chinese categories, exploring how Buddhist terminology might be used to portray Christ, beginning a Christian dialogue with Buddhist monks. Whether or not, as some have argued, their work had permanent effect within Buddhism itself, promoting the hope of a merciful saviour that developed in China, (so different from the original teaching of the Buddha) it is clear that they entered on an intellectual project as daring as that of Paul and Justin and Origen.

Or we could turn south, and follow the early planting of the Christian faith in Africa. Early Ethiopian Christianity, while resolutely confronting the territorial spirits known to African village society, developed its own distinctive literature and tradition of scholarship, using its own distinctive writing system. In the course of its tumultuous history, the recurrent revivals of the Ethiopian church and the recovery of Ethiopian Christianity from near disaster have been accompanied by a revival of scholarship; often in forbidding conditions. Scholarship has never been an easy path in Ethiopia; the fearless evangelists of its classical period had learned to copy a manuscript while sitting on a narrow ledge above a deep precipice.

The point is equally made by the early Western Christianity that grew up among the people the Romans called barbarians. Scholars such as Isidore of Seville and Bede of England used the cultural resources of the peoples of northern and western Europe to extend Christian thinking, producing historical writing of a new type–evangelistic history, one might almost call it–that related national history to the story of salvation. Scholars reflecting on issues that arose out of thinking Christian themes together with traditional law and custom, strengthened by the widespread adoption of the styles of Roman law, opened the way for a deepened understanding of sin, judgment and atonement. What made this flowering of scholarship possible was a modification of some of the missionary structures of the church to embrace the task of scholarship. The monasteries, always nurseries of the devotional life, and in early northern Europe important as evangelistic bases, became centres of co-operative scholarship.

Or, moving to more recent times, we could consider the missionary movement from the West. When it began, Christianity had become thoroughly accommodated to Western culture, and in a process extending over centuries had penetrated deep into its thought, its customs, its laws, its art and literature. For long centuries Western Christians were largely cut off from most of the non-Western world. From the sixteenth century onwards they were massively in contact with it, and the inadequacies of the Western intellectual tradition for coping with this new world were manifest. They were particularly manifest to those who wanted to communicate the word about Christ. At first it seemed a matter mainly of language; communication of the Gospel would be easy once missionaries could speak the languages of Africa and Asia. It was not long before it became plain that language is only the outer skin of the consciousness we now call culture. The Gospel had to pass beyond language into the depths of a consciousness that had taken centuries to form and which now shaped the way people thought and acted.

The missionary movement introduced a new element into Western Christian experience. A very sure-footed, confident Christianity with centuries of cultural interaction behind it had to make its way in other people's terms; terms that at the time were only vaguely comprehended, and seemed alien if not repellent. Western Christianity came to Asia and Africa assured about its own tradition of learning, and then found that tradition had huge gaps; vast areas where the Western Academy, theological or secular, had nothing useful to say. The missionary movement, out of its essential concern to communicate the Gospel, was forced into innovative scholarship. Missionaries Catholic from the early days, Protestant afterwards turned Western scholarship in new directions. New disciplines or fields of study were invented or made possible: in the languages and literatures of the world beyond Europe, in comparative linguistics, in anthropology, and comparative religion and tropical medicine. The Western Academy in its present secular phase has forgotten where these things came from. They arose, or were made possible, by the desire that Christ should be known in other cultures.

Here then is our starting place: that Christian history indicates that searching, fundamental scholarship arises naturally out of the exercise of Christian mission and especially from its cross-cultural expression. Mission involves moving out of one's self and one's accustomed terrain, and taking the risk of entering another world. It means living on someone else's terms. As the Gospel itself is about God living on someone else's terms, the Word becoming flesh, Divinity being expressed in terms of humanity. And the transmission of the Gospel requires a process analogous, however distantly, to that great act on which Christian faith depends. Cross-cultural diffusion (which is the life blood of historic Christianity) has to go beyond language, the outer skin of culture, into the processes of thinking and choosing and all the networks of relationship that lie beneath language, turning then all towards Christ. It requires generations to accomplish, for those processes have themselves taken many generations to form. This is *deep* translation, the appropriation of the Christian Gospel in terms of that culture, down to the very roots of identity. Periods of active mission need to be periods of active scholarship. The converse is also true; when the sense of mission is dulled or diverted, the death knell sounds for Christian scholarship.

## 15.
## Hip-Hop and the Black Church: In Search for mutual embracing

By Charles Howard
*formerly student of* Andover Newton Theological School

The minimal conversation that has occurred between the Black Church and Hip-Hop (both creations of the African-Americans), is nothing less than a failure. It is a failure because these two emblems that define cultural creations have encountered missed opportunities in their conversation and manifested strong attitudes of mutual exclusion. Amongst the main disappointments is the lack of willingness to learn from each other, along with the fact that they both are the voice of the marginalized.

The purpose of this essay is to place an emergency call upon the members of these two 'orders' to encourage them to enter into conversation with one another. First, I will examine several similarities between the two, including their common shortcomings. Secondly, I will seek to find new venues so that they can learn from each other and edify each other, and why not increase the awareness for the need of a prophetic voice.

Hip-Hop culture is about self-definition and shaking off the labels that are forced upon by certain members of our society. Yet, one attempting to define Hip-Hop might begin with Rap music. Rap music is a cultural expression, where through rhymed lyrics, the artist tells his story, making Rap a way of preserving memory. It is usually accompanied by highly rhythmic, electronically based music that adds to the desired effect of the song. Rap became popular during the 1970's, built upon the older forms of art as Bebop of jazz, Black radio DJ's, Blues singers, and the drum music of Africa. It is widely accepted that Rap began in South Bronx, NY as apart of the growing Hip-Hop cultural movement of the time. Tricia Rose, in her influential book *Black Noise* writes that "Rap music is black cultural expression that prioritizes black voices from the margins of Urban America [...] From the outset, Rap music has articulated the pleasures and problems of Black urban life in contemporary America."

Although an African-American creation, Hip-Hop is still a 'Diaspora phenomenon' for the people of African decent, since it profits from a major Latino/Hispanic strand. This is so because of Latino's sharing of the same peripheral seat with African Americans in the United States. Ironically, today people of all backgrounds and socio-economic positions have at least one foot in the room of Hip-Hop culture.

I believe that in any conversation about "What the African-American must do," the Hip-Hop element must be invited to the table beside the Black Church. At this year's Academy of Music Awards (Grammys) the president of the academy said, "Rap music is the CNN of inner city urban life." For unquestionable reasons, Hip-Hop is already the voice of the African-American and, at times of oppression, is perhaps the loudest one. Where else could the struggle against oppression and racism be heard? The media has the tendency to create the picture that the African Americans are happy and do well in business. Some media tendencies display the majority of the blacks as "funny minstrels" on the air. The televised sporting events show pictures implying that the only way that the blacks can be famous is by being athletic, or by doing something that will get them on the 11:00 news in hand cuffs.

A poignant similarity between Hip-Hop and the Black Church that justifies their commonality is the male dominance structure. I remember during a lecture to a high school, I have asked the students to name as many male rappers as they could and they continued to yell out names for over five minutes. When I asked them to name female rappers they could only name 4. I asked them to name female DJs and they could not name one. Apparently, this is not because they are less educated about female emcees and DJs; it is rather because of the reality that there aren't very many of them. Also women in Rap are not marketed as well and have a much more difficult time in the industry compared to their male counterparts. Here, sexism becomes as realistic as concerning. It is exemplified in the objectification of women in music videos and even lyrics. The premier female lyricists like Bahamadia and the Brat are often given a back seat to other rappers who show their bodies and Rap about sexual issues. Moreover, sexism is more rampant on the male side and shown in vicious, sometime violent lyrics toward women, introducing them as elements of entertainment. It is important to note that it cannot only be the writers and producers who receive the blame, but also those who buy and request this type of songs.

Speaking of gender issue in the Black Church it is to be observed that even now, most of black denominational conferences easily reveal that vast majority of church leadership is male, while the vast majority of membership is female. It is not uncommon to enter a church and see a male pastor preaching to rows and rows of women with few men scattered among them.

Other similarities between the Black Church and Hip-Hop are their diversities of ethnic make up, economic and social status. None of the two is monolithic. Despite the social similarities between Hip-Hop and the Black Church, it is often that the Church casts harsh criticism upon Rap, when in fact, sociologically, the church preserves a similar cliché, on gender structure.

The African influence in both the Black Church as well as Rap music and dance must be paid homage. The worship style in black churches could not have been that way without its African ancestry. Likewise, the Hip Hop is what it is because of its African ancestry.

The prophetic call for a mutual embracing between Hip-Hop culture and Black Church remains one aspect that urgently needs consideration all the more as the contemporary global tendencies increasingly create opportunities for self-expression of African-American culture. Hip-Hop and the Black Church can share their prophetic vision with each other in regaining their common force. They both interpret reality and voice it out through their own means. In the global village, the Hip-Hop reality is preached through records, it is worn on clothes, and written on the walls. It is because of this shared path that the ears of Rap artists, graffiti artistes, those who speak with their hands on the tables, and those who dance to the beats, must be opened for conversation with the church.

# 16.
## *Global Vision and Religious Conviction:*
## *An Orthodox Christian Reflection on Globalization*

By George C. Papademetriou
Holy Cross Greek Orthodox School of Theology

The question the lawyer addressed to Jesus Christ, "Who is my neighbor?" (Luke 10: 29) now has a new dimension. The neighbor is not only the one who lives next door, but also the one who lives across the ocean. The sense of distance has been redefined by modern technology. The world has shrunk with the growth of travel telecommunications, and the instant dissemination of information regarding events everywhere in the world. Globalization brings all cultures and civilizations into the "public square."

The "Attack on America on September 11, 2001, points to the negative aspects of globalization. In that case, there was a clash of cultures, and globally available technology assisted in making that clash destructive and horribly deadly.

The survival of world human community requires cooperation among the adherents of all religions. The objective of globalization in religious terms must be the synergy of adherents of all religions to attain peaceful coexistence. The technological impact on the world economy is of great importance in economic globalization, but this should not give us the illusion of peaceful coexistence. Political situations, war and peace, economics, human rights, and justice compels religious persons to move closer to the center of visionary implementation of God's love in the world of suffering and injustice.

Peaceful coexistence is accomplished by building relationships among religious persons of all faiths and working together for the benefit of humankind. Religious adherents must share the divine love and be open to the spirit of God. It is empathy and compassion that brings people together.

All persons of good faith condemn evil, and proclaim love and peace. These religious values play significant roles and become powerful symbols in determining inter-human relations.

One role of Orthodox Christianity in the global village is that which it has been for 2,000 years, to balance the political and economic resources to achieve social justice for all people. Christianity is a universal vehicle through which multicultural and multi-religious societies live in harmony and respect for each other. Christianity is not an ideology but a way of life and sacramental experience. Christianity must recreate the social order to what our world should look like and become a model of relations of all people. The resurgence of Orthodox Christianity with the breakup of the former Soviet Union, and the revival of the Orthodox consciousness of a universal unity and cooperation, is evident in the connection of the Orthodox people everywhere.

Globalization must not destroy diverse religious and cultural identities in exchange for economic and political control. It must be checked by the traditional, well-founded religious values fostering world order, justice, and peaceful coexistence of all people and religions.

## 17.
## *Education for Globalization?*

By Robert W. Pazmiño
Andover Newton Theological School

Globalization calls us to recognize that we occupy one world and represent one race, the human race, who share a common lot with all of creation. With all that divides humanity and defaces God's creation, the question of our legacy for future generations is essential to raise in relation to the survival of our global community. Bernard Bailyn defined education as "the entire process by which a culture transmits itself across the generations."[1] The legacy we are passing on to the seventh generation is a concern of Amerindian peoples. It is also a concern I increasingly experience as my wife and I look forward to becoming grandparents for the first time next May. The Christian tradition among others recognizes our accountability and responsibility before God. The fruits of the creed of greed and consumption promoted by many suggest the need for radical alternatives, radical in the sense of a return to our common roots.

Education for globalization calls for posing questions and problems. Questions are posed in terms of the active discovery of a common good for the commonwealth of creation. Problems are posed in terms of the global ecological crisis that jeopardizes all of life. The Gospel of Jesus Christ proclaims good news regarding one who "is the image of the invisible God, the firstborn of all creation; for in him all things in heaven and on earth were created, things visible and invisible, whether thrones or dominions or rulers or powers—all things created through him and for him. He himself is before all things, and in him all things hold together." (Colossians 1:15-17, NRSV)

---

[1] Bernard Bailyn, *Education in the Forming of American Society.* (New York: W.W. Norton, 1960), 14.

The Christmas message to the shepherds noted "good news of great joy for all the people." (Luke 2:10) What good news of joy can be heard for all people in our global context and shared with my grandchild? The demands of righteousness, justice, and peace require an agenda that transcends the divisions of generations, gender, class, culture, ethnicity, and religious and ideological persuasion. The radical message of Jesus Christ embraces both an education for Christian identity in the light of the cross and suffering, and an education for hospitality and openness to our neighbors who affirm other religious perspectives.

Embracing a call for global educational vision requires a willingness to incarnate that vision in how we live personally, communally and corporately. It also requires the risks of modeling and mentoring for the rising generations what we have readily only hoped they might live out in the future. We have much to learn from Generations X, Y and Z regarding where the gaps exist between our vision and realities and what alternatives can be explored. Middle age adults in particular are called to have a teachable spirit in exploring what new frontiers globalization invites all of us to cross in considering where we are going in the third millennium. Education in and for faith within our global setting requires us to honor God as our teacher in both old and new ways.[2] God delights to reveal God's will through the gracious working of God's Spirit despite our best and often limited efforts of the past. These are lessons I hope to pass on to my grandchild and to share globally "not leaving any child behind."

---

[2] See my discussion in *God Our Teacher: Theological Basics in Christian Education* (Grand Rapids: Baker, 2001) and "Surviving or Thriving in the Third Millennium?" in *Forging a Better Religious Education in the Third Millennium*, ed. James M. Lee (Birmingham, Ala: Religious Education Press, 2000), 69-88.

## 18.
## *Religion and Conflict as Global Concern*

By Raymond G. Helmick, S.J.
Boston College Department of Theology

Religion as a resource or problem for global order, much less peace, requires a word of caution at the outset. It is not that religion has too often proven a negative factor, though that is often true and needs analysis and discussion; but rather that one ought not look to religion for purposes other than its own. The point of this article is to look, first, to the purposes of religion and, then, to its role in global social order.

A religious faith is in itself an all-encompassing outlook on life, on the world and its meaning. It generates its own agenda, and reluctant though we may be, we must allow it to do that. Outsiders who try to utilize religion for their own purposes may have good or bad agendas of their own. Even those of us who regard ourselves as insiders to a faith community may yield to the temptation of using religion for an extraneous purpose. People who look to religion as a help in resolving conflicts always feel they have the best motives anyone might think of. But it is always an abuse of religious faith to make it instrument for something else.

There are of course some other potential reasons for this tarnishing of the religious record in areas of conflict. Besides this extrinsic cause, the instrumental use of religion, there may be intrinsic stimuli to the rejection and exclusion of others, and the licensing of violence against them: concepts of divine revelation or election that establish sharp separation between the recipients of God's word, or the elect, and the reprobate or unbelievers. Or great harm may be done by concepts of an angry, vengeful God, in whose service we may visit wrath upon our enemies.

All governments have caught on to the fact that churches are the custodians of Just War theory. When the war begins, every government appeals at once to the church to get up in the cheering section and proclaim that "God is on our side." We never belong there. Our role as proclaimers of *shalom* demands of us that we be searching actively for alternatives to violence. But we have all seen churches fall right into the trap and preach national exclusivism and God's wrath, as if they were qualified to declare it, upon the enemy.

We expect that commitment to reconciliation to characterize any of the faith communities. They seem to be strong in theory, weak in practice of that quality. I speak from within a community of Christian faith, which has great importance to me. I've seen the working of several other faith communities, understood something of their theological positions and the concrete practice of their commitments. I won't try to speak for them on this subject of reconciliation, but commend, to those of you who live in those other traditions, to examine teaching and practice in this matter of reconciliation within them and explain it to the rest of us.

Within my Christian context, nothing has greater theoretical priority. The Christian Gospel accounts abound in summonses to reconciliation, perhaps nowhere more imperatively than in *Matthew* 5, 23-24: "If you are offering your gift at the altar, and there remember that your brother has something against you, leave your gift there before the altar and go; first be reconciled with your brother, and then come and offer your gift." Ritual practice can wait, and has no importance comparable to that of reconciliation.

In practice, Christian history has shown us a lot of concern with justice, consistently retributive justice. We hear far less of reconciliation or the practice of forgiveness that the Gospels so much urge. But a peculiar thing happened to the practice of reconciliation in Christian history. It disappeared into the confessional and became exclusively forgiveness of sin by God.

In this way it was privatized, made exclusively a matter between me and Jesus. Reconciliation with the brother, the sister, the neighbor tended to be lost in the shuffle. Especially the public character of reconciliation and forgiveness, the reestablishment of wholeness in the relations between nations and peoples, failed to become a focus in the life of the faith community. Concepts of retribution and compulsion reigned supreme in all those public areas.

We may have the impression, after the troubles of more recent years, that a determined effort was made to retract that recognition of the other people's legitimacy. If so, the good news is that it proved impossible. Such a solemn recognition, once granted, could not be rescinded, and the seeds of peace once planted have survived to be watered once again.

Many of us have a very particular interest in the theme of restorative justice, as much a social as a religious issue. It has its importance within the legal system or in any striving for international peace, in the resolution or transformation of conflicts. In our country this has become an important concern among a broad range of lawyers and judges, who have seen the purely retributive system characteristic of our practice of justice as poisoning our society with a cult of vengeance.

The concept needs grounding in the wisdom traditions, something we may seek in the various faith communities. Without that, the work undertaken will likely amount to no more than tinkering with the legal system, and will fall short of the profound transformation it could make in out society.

## 19.
# From Faith to Illusion:
# An Orthodox Christian Response to Buddhist
# Philosophy on the Quest of Mental Suffering

By Marian Gh. Simion
Boston Theological Institute

This age of advanced technology and ultra-rapid communications provides us with the odd and often unexpected surprise that young people– Orthodox Christians in particular–seem to embrace an increasing curiosity for Buddhist spirituality. It seems so, perhaps, because of the restless search for more material venues in regaining physical rejuvenation and beauty, as well as for alleviating physical pain and spiritual affliction; needs that revolve around the marketing system of a pseudo-medicine.

Here I would like to provide an analysis of the tools that are used by Orthodox Christians and Buddhists in healing spiritual ailments and to highlight their theological meaning. Secondarily, I would like to offer guidelines for Orthodox Christians, to assist in their understanding of Buddhist spiritual methodologies on therapeutic sophistication – so much aroused by the New Age complexity – as well as to try to set some boundaries around their risky curiosity.

A curious Orthodox Christian, more or less grounded in his home faith, finds out that the spiritual methods of yoga, for instance, seem to provide more definite methodological trajectories for mental excitement, emotional balance and physical strength. Moreover, when confronted with emotional distress, the philosophy that constitutes the 'requited' companion to such practices, provides the sufferer with a surprising worldview, which denies rather than acknowledges everything that exists. In fact, only few adherents of the Buddhist practices are aware that the Buddha taught a total denial of all existence. In this situation, a person in emotional distress and in need of being recognized as a person appeals to the Buddhist 'spirituality' and finds out that he comes to the point where he must deny everything. He denies himself, he denies God, the human soul and affirms that everything is but a mental construction. "According to Buddhism," says Walpola Rahula, "our ideas of God and Soul are false and empty. Though highly developed as theories, they are all the same extremely subtle mental projections, garbed in an intricate metaphysical and philosophical phraseology." (Walpola 1974: 52)

Aiming for a passionate outreach not just for the meaning but also for the roots of suffering, Buddhist philosophy–concentrated around the teachings of the Buddha ('the Enlightened One') – makes a strong claim that it has found the 'medicine' to cure the spiritual ailment (Dolly 1965: 72-95). For a Buddhist, the total negation of all existence, along with the dilemma of its redefinition as illusory, appears to be just a formulation amongst the many. Nevertheless, the intentional construction of loneliness, combined with the atheistic presuppositions for living, come to the point of abolishing any sort of dialogic engagement with a Supra-Existential Being, however that might be understood. Perhaps the only 'positive' side of Buddhist strategy is that questions on suffering, which are never satisfied by any potential answer, are better off if never addressed. It is positive only to the extent that God answered Job's unjustified suffering with silence. In this context, it is not necessary to consider the question itself, as such, since everything is unreal and represents but the outcome of a simple mental projection.

The Buddhist paradox is that the quest for an answer is nonetheless a desire for knowledge, a desire to make a meaning out of a situation. A question such as 'why there is pain in the world' – implying a form of desire for answer – is destroyed by a statement such as: "the first cause of pain is desire" (Percheron 1957: 49), offering therefore a self-contradictory answer. "Buddha's every sermon or simple dialogue," says Maurice Percheron, "is heading back to the main of existence, and to the causes of suffering. He frequently dwells on the harmful illusion of thinking what is impermanent to be fixed, of relying on appearances, which have nothing to do with reality – if reality even exists." (Percheron 1957: 50)

Does Orthodox Christian theology avoid the quest of suffering? Certainly, not. On the contrary, Christian theology is constantly seeking dialogue, even a silent one. A Christian never avoids questioning unjust suffering. Even Jesus Christ, when unjustly bruised, asked for justification by saying: "If I have spoke evil, bear witness of the evil; but if well, why do you strike Me?" (John 18:20) An Orthodox Christian interrogates God about suffering, *because* he puts his trust in Him. A convinced Buddhist does not have to ask this question because he does not have a 'god' to ask. He rather believes that the mind is the only place to work out suffering. Ceasing to think of suffering will end suffering (Walshe 1963: 55-6). Moreover, a convinced Buddhist believes that he might become free only if he renounces the desire for an answer to the quest of suffering and detaches himself from any form of curiosity and desire. In the Christian understanding, the desire for answer, is not, as the Buddha states, an evil, but an immense power for healing any form of alienation, through communion with God and with all cosmic existence.

In identifying the cause of suffering, Buddhist philosophy uses a syllogistic construct. Thus, the first cause of suffering *desire*, the second is *lack of self-control*, and the third one is *ignorance* in the way that there is a demonstrated refusal or disregard of knowledge (Percheron 1957: 49-50).

In the Christian understanding there is no syllogistic method in giving rationales for the origin and cause of suffering. A Christian might simply state that pain and suffering originate in the act of breaking communion with God, and they outline the consequence of original sin, which despite an apparent simplicity, constitutes a very abstruse issue. Communion with God is a profound proposition of living meditation. It involves every aspect of human existence from rational thinking, through feelings, moral standards, non-exiled human relationships, uncontaminated sharing and incommensurable love as expressed in the liturgy. A convinced Buddhist teaches cessation of suffering through a redefinition of relationship, which, despite the communal practicality–quite visible in the Buddhist monastic setting–negates every attachment towards any human fellowship.

The purpose of a guru-apprentice relationship is only utilitarian, rather than being anchored in communal love. A Buddhist guru is someone whose only task is rational 'illumination.' A Christian spiritual father, on the other hand, is someone holding a power given from above as to go straight to the essence of suffering, to heal and forgive the sin which has alienated the spiritual son from his communion with the Heavenly Father (Matthew 18: 18).

The two opposite notions of good and evil seem to enshrine the hypothesis, or even perhaps the cause of suffering. To this extent, the Christian and the Buddhist perceptions are again unmatchable and clearly distinct from one another, despite their sociological similarities.

The Buddhist concepts of good and evil are encapsulated exclusively into the human act. There is basically no existential good or evil, except to the extent of considering the human act as good or evil. "The conceptions of good and evil are personal as much as altruistic," says Maurice Percheron. "Evil is the satisfaction of a desire; it is wrong done to the others. Good, on the other hand, implies a personal sacrifice along with respect for every mind, and likewise for every life, even that of an enemy. Here we have the doctrine of non-violence (*ahimsa*) assumption of an inner un-assailability' as a defense against evil."(Percheron 1957: 67) It is, therefore, very clear that good and evil for a Buddhist are only human acts, while for a Christian, good is an instinct emanating from God's love, while evil is only an accident of breaking communion with God. A convinced Buddhist does the good and the evil out of exercise, so as to experience detachment from the sense of property and from a prosaic self-awareness. Because of these standards, doing good for the other fellow human being is far from being an act of charity and love. The Buddhist understanding of charity, as Maurice Percheron explains, "will be neither a sentimental act of helping one's neighbor, nor following the Indian conception, and act of devotion to divinity. It marks one step in the stony path of personal detachment." It does not testify towards an acceptance of a brotherhood made of love, but rather a slightly condescending benevolence towards what belongs to the human species. "Let no one forget his own duty for the sake of another's, however great: let a man, after he has discerned his own duty, be always attentive to his duty."(Percheron 1957: 68)

It is, therefore, a very clear egoism. It is never an affirmation and recognition of the other, but a denial. Moreover, it is not only a denial of the other, but much more, since it goes to the denial of one's self. "It is undeniable," points out Maurice Percheron, "that the negation of the soul as a salting entity, the rejection of an accessible God, the very idea of karmic transmigration could not but horrify a convinced Christian."(Percheron 1957: 166) Therefore, in the Buddhist act of healing suffering, there is an impenetrable wall between the sufferer and the healer. A relationship constructed upon a theological understanding of love and existential compassion can never be achieved. Even modern methods of psychotherapy acknowledge that, in the act of healing, it is always a need for recognition and affirmation of the self-image of the patient. For a Christian, recognizing the other is the outcome of unconditional love, which the one in need of healing needs. A Christian can never reconcile the act of loving the other with the act of denying the other.

I have addressed this topic, because it appears to me that young people today–especially those from western societies–manifest an increasing interest in oriental spirituality and place themselves in a dangerous trap of naively accepting that Buddhist philosophy holds a monopoly upon resolving the quest of suffering. For me this 'faith' is but a delusion if not a new form of atheism, which is far superior to Marx's conceptualization of religion as a human invention. It is, I believe, a trap seductively attractive because of the lack of awareness of what the treasury of Orthodox Christian spirituality can provide, associated with an obvious sense of curiosity and search for spiritual adventure. Despite an apparent compassion towards all sentient beings, Buddhist philosophy entrenches human alienation, along with a delusive act of relationship. Healing love, which can only become realistic in the presence of the other, reveals the strength of Christian faith, always available in the church and yet to be discovered. Although sometimes positive and beneficial for mental balance and physical health, Buddhist methodologies, concentrated around yoga practices, are very dangerous, because they negate God and the human soul, reducing them to simply mental actions. In this way they increase the sense of loneliness and alienation from God and human community. God becomes a prosaic and old-fashioned religious notion, inactive and inaccessible to the 'post-modern' person.

Therefore, someone attempting to heal emotional distress by giving total credit to Buddhist methods, may do so only by negating and losing God along with all his fellow human beings. That person becomes a self-imposed island maintaining a distorted sense of relationship. Healing requires a liturgical engagement of God and the human community. Compassion and presence makes suffering easier and more hopeful. Only such compassionate presence of others can make the burden of pain lighter and easier to bear.

**Sources Consulted:**

*The Orthodox Study Bible: New Testament and Psalms*. (New King James Version) Thomas Nelson Publishers, Nashville, Tennessee, 1993.

Bowker, John. *Oxford Dictionary of World Religions*. Oxford University Press: New York, 1997.

Facter, Dolly. *The Doctrine of the Buddha*. Philosophical Library: New York, 1965.

Percheron, Maurice. *Buddha and Buddhism*. Harper & Brothers: New York, 1957.

Rahula, Walpola. *What the Buddha Taught*. Grove Press: New York, 1974.

Walshe, M.O'C. *Buddhism for Today*. Philosophical Library: New York, 1963.

# 20.
# *Dignity Matters*

By Donna Hicks
Harvard University

*What do you think is required by the field of conflict resolution to address the complexity of the current situation we are facing in the international arena?*

I believe that we need to pay closer attention to the human dimension of conflict–to the effect that it has on the inner world of human beings. One of the contributions of our work at PICAR has been to bring the issue of human needs into the political discourse about conflict–a discourse that has been historically dominated by the language of power, interests, and the state. While recognizing the importance and inevitability of the use of the paradigm of realpolitik to frame our thinking about conflict and its resolution, we have argued that the social-psychological perspective–the framework from which the human needs approach emerged–is one that can be viewed as a complement to power politics, though by no means a substitute. It is but one dimension of the multitude of variables that contributes to the complexity that is inherent to the analysis of conflict.

The fundamental assumption of the human needs approach is that when their basic need for dignity is threatened, humans will react violently, if necessary, to restore it. Dignity is derived from fulfilling the need for identity, security, belonging, recognition, and justice. These needs are inviolable and cannot be negotiated away. No amount of power can suppress the desire to have the needs fulfilled. An army may eliminate the cadres fighting for the restoration of the needs, but it cannot eliminate the powerful human yearning to live one's life in dignity.

The main point here is to recognize another source of power. Power that is defined not by the strength of armies, sophistication of weapons, or the control of resources, but by the capacity of the human spirit to overcome even the most primal of human instincts – the instinct of self-preservation–in the service of the restoration of human dignity.

*How do you think this concern should influence domestic and international discourse relating to the events of September 11th and their aftermath?*

At this juncture, as we continue to search for an understanding of the conditions that created the human tragedy that was brought on by the attacks of September 11th we are at an optimal moment in which to examine the importance of the "human dimension" of these events. That a small group of individuals had the capacity to inflict so much harm and devastation on the most powerful country in the world by such unconventional means–by engaging the power of the human spirit to overcome the fear of death for a higher calling–warrants our attention. In so doing, I am attempting to extend the analysis beyond this particular case of September 11th to the consequences of ignoring the human dimension in international politics in general.

Although I am fully aware and accepting of the many arguments that have been made to explain the motivation behind the behavior of the perpetrators of the attacks of September 11th ranging from the role of the internal oppressive conditions of many Arab states to the role of United States foreign policy in the Middle East *vis a vis* the Palestinian-Israeli conflict, I suggest that it would be a mistake to dismiss the importance of the perception of a sustained threat to the dignity of those responsible for the attacks.

It is well documented in the literature of psychology that human beings often react to a threat to their well being with a defensive response. Daniel Goleman, in his book *Emotional Intelligence*, describes how the old brain (limbic system) becomes activated by threat, essentially taking over the activities of the neo-cortex, which is the part of the brain responsible for rational thought. These often violent, defensive behaviors that are triggered by threat include a desire for attack, revenge and justice. And it is not only a physical threat that can trigger such a response. James Gilligan, in his book *Violence,* argues that a psychological threat to one's dignity – such as repeated experiences of humiliation–has the capacity to motivate some of the most heinous acts of violence. According to Gilligan, one of the best-kept secrets about the human condition is the extent to which we will avoid, at all costs, the experience of feeling humiliated and diminished. The power behind these defensive reactions – reactions that protect the challenged dignity of those threatened–is incalculable.

What I am suggesting is that those who organized and carried out the attacks of September 11th were reacting, in part, to the perception–whether real or imagined – that the United States is a threat to the dignity of the Arab world and more generally to Islam. In their minds, the U.S. policy in the Middle East has brought about the suffering of and injustice to the Palestinian people by not speaking out against Israel's oppressive policies in the West Bank and Gaza. Added to that is their concern that the spread of American influence and culture throughout the Muslim world threatens their fundamental identity as Muslims, as well their way of life. By linking these threats to their dignity to a fanatical interpretation of Islam, which enabled them to murder innocent citizens of the world – albeit mostly US citizens – they justified a most cruel act of inhumanity in the service of a higher calling.

The main point is that we cannot afford to ignore what is happening at the human level in international politics. The effects of our actions, motivated predominantly by self-interest, will incite consequences at the human level that would normally be considered irrelevant to international politics. The conceptualization of power in international discourse needs to acknowledge the power of the human spirit to commit the most unthinkable acts of inhumanity when provoked by a threat to dignity. One does not even need to argue this from a moral perspective. It is sufficient to say that on pragmatic grounds it is not in the interest of any government to violate the dignity not only of their own people but also of any other people within the international community.

The effects of humiliation can travel far beyond national borders. The way we treat one another matters, whether the unit of analysis is international politics or interpersonal relations. Violating the dignity of human beings has its consequences. The question is whether we want to live in a world where we must be constantly at the ready for the next big threat or, rather, that we tap into another qualitatively different form of strength, which is the strength that it takes to overcome the power of the cycle of rage, revenge, and retaliation. The strength that it takes to restrain the instinctive impulse to fight back requires an internal source of power that weapons and armies cannot touch. It is this often untapped and underused strength that we are capable of as humans, that could unleash courage and restraint rather than rage and shift the destructive dynamics in which we are currently entangled.

*How do you suggest that Americans begin to remedy the situation in which we find ourselves?*

While acknowledging the need to protect ourselves during this time of crisis, I suggest that it behooves us to think carefully about developing a new relationship to power. As the world's greatest superpower, defined in conventional terms, we could choose to tap into that other source of strength – that would enable us to put an end to the cycle of violence and develop policies both home and abroad that are genuinely committed to preserving the dignity of all human beings. This new relationship to power would require a level of awareness and acceptance of the impact of our actions on one another and force us to examine closely the consequences of policies that are driven by self-interest alone. This new relationship to power would require us to develop the capacity for empathy for those who are less fortunate than we, especially for those who are trapped in human suffering as a consequence of abuses of power and domination by one group over another. It would require an awareness of the power of including others in one's analysis of interests; the power of acknowledging injustice rather than turning a blind eye to it; the power of recognizing, accepting, and taking responsibility for one's blind spots and the harmful consequences of them on others. This new relationship to power would give us the moral courage to make the choices that would bring out the best rather than the worst in one another. And I would argue that the "best" is yet to come, that we have only begun to explore what we are capable of, guided by a balanced view of both the privileges and responsibilities that power brings.

Paradoxically, the greatest privilege that power provides is the opportunity to use it in the service of the restoration of humanity, for to preserve it for the benefit of the few at the expense of the many only trap us in the self-centered illusion that what matters to us, alone, is the only thing that counts. This awareness opens us up to the yet to be explored possibility that, by bringing out the best in one another, we can get down to the business of flourishing as human beings rather than expending all of our resources and energy on protecting ourselves from the next big threat. And the good news is that all we have to do is find the courage to make the choice.

*The interview was conducted by Dr. Rodney L. Petersen,*
*Executive Director of the Boston Theological Institute*

## 21.
## *What is Church Responsible to do about Conflicts?*

By Raymond G. Helmick, SJ
Boston College Department of Theology

As we celebrate the World Council's *Decade to Overcome Violence*, we can hardly ignore the extent to which religion has actually fomented violence, historically and in the conflicts of our time, with Christian churches not at all behind other faith traditions in this destructive work. Our churches, over much of our history, have ill served the mission of reconciliation, which our Gospel requires with such priority. How do we account for this?

One fashionable explanation regards religion as essentially ambivalent with regard to good or evil. Scott Appleby's recent and valuable book, *The Ambivalence of the Sacred*, accepts this hypothesis, basing it on Rudolph Otto's classic (1917) definition of "The Holy" as *"mysterium tremendum et fascinans."* For Otto, the numinous quality of the sacred, combined with the dread evoked by its overpowering presence, could motivate irrational responses, for good or evil. We have to recognize an inadequacy of this concept of the holy to describe the object of our faith, as it applies just as well to the ancient idols of wood or stone, or the distracting idolatries of our contemporary world, as it does to the God who reveals himself as healer and calls us to reconciliation.

Our faith, though, has lent itself frequently to cooptation. Church and churches have let themselves be commandeered by agendas foreign to their own, agendas of states or parties, of self-aggrandizing nationalism, of the expression of rage by those who feel themselves oppressed. As soon as faith expresses itself in institutional form it acquires interests to be preserved: the safety of its community which, if it does not conform to the world about it, could be threatened by turbulent or dominating forces; the freedom of its institutional functions; things as mundane as the maintenance of its physical property. All of these constitute motives for serving purposes which have nothing to do with the agenda of faith. Everyone has long realized, for instance, that churches have a real degree of custody over just war theory. In the event of war, nations call upon their churches to get up in the cheering section and pronounce that "God is on our side." Churches resist this only with great difficulty. They never belong there, but should always question the war, putting it and its conduct relentlessly to the test of justice.

Such cooptation showed itself in the wars of the former Yugoslavia, where both Orthodox and Catholic senses of identity were utilized by the opposing forces to rationalize appalling atrocities against one another and especially against the weaker Muslims. Rare are the heroes, like Serbian Orthodox Patriarch Pavle, who have stood firm against that tide. In Irish history, ever since the Reformation, Catholic or Protestant allegiance has served as the political loyalty test of contending nationalisms. Examples abound, and I confine myself here to the Christian examples. Other religions suffer this syndrome as much.

All those instances, though, remain external to the faith itself. In other cases, distortions internal to the expression of faith may also lead to exclusion, often with cruelty, of others as unfit, unblessed, unworthy of the full dignity of human persons. In this regard we all have to look to our teachings on revelation and election. Every religion, in fact, has these doctrines in some form, benign or dangerous. We could spend some time on these, but I will confine myself to pointing out that Ernst Troeltsch served us all well in giving these exclusivisms the name of sectarianism. The churches in Ireland have produced some of the most valuable study of this phenomenon in their sectarianism project.

Our Christian churches fell together into this trap at the time of the Reformation, seeking ways to condemn and refute each other rather than to understand and validate one another's Christian faith. We may argue that the European constituencies of the various churches, and their American descendants, became alienated from their own religious institutions as a result of the religious wars of the 16th and 17th centuries. Since the time of the peace of Westphalia, public profession of atheism or agnosticism has become the commonplace of intellectual discourse, and a much wider public in these countries greets all claims of institutional privilege of their churches with instinctive distrust. The Christian churches have alienated their own constituencies by their tendency to violence.

No tendency among peoples of faith carries more potential for deadly conflict than this exclusivism. We can deal with it through a culture of tolerance, recognizing freedom of conscience for those of faiths other than our own. If we would go further and recognize legitimacy in other faiths or other formulae even of our own Christian faith, we raise, in every case, the problem of whether we can recognize authentic action of God in others' faith without betrayal of our own. This is an especially important area if we are to overcome the potential for violence in religious conflict, and brings risks, which we must confront, of relativizing our own expression of faith. The experience of interfaith dialogue in our own time has opened possibilities that are still very new to most of us.

As violent and as discouraging as has been the performance of churches and religions through history, we encounter a new level of menace in our own time in the form of religious fundamentalism.

Our use of the term has only recently gained some clarity, largely as the result of the extensive and quite noble work of Scott Appleby and Martin Marty. Prior to their work we had to keep reminding ourselves that the term's primary use was in describing the biblical literalism of some American churches in the 19th and 20th centuries and that it was not properly used in other contexts. But while that earlier use of the expression referred first to the literalism of biblical interpretation, the principal trait we signal by it now is the fundamentalist's determination to impose a form of religious observance on others.

We have known religious coercion for a long time. Just recently I reread the *acta* of the famous trial of Galileo and realized the level of submission and self-abasement required of this victim of the Inquisition, characteristic of the proceedings of that institution, whose work was duplicated in many other churches, not least in the early Christian churches of this region of New England. It has always had to do with assertion of the power of institutions. But in recent times it has arisen in new contexts.

The fundamentalism we see now occurs in the setting of a secularized world. What is it? A group, often young, who see the chaos of the current world in terms of the failure of the culture to live by religious precept, draws the conclusion the religious conformity must be imposed by force. Usually the outward signs of this conformity will be very visible: a way of dress, manners of behavior, requirement of beards, headdress, etc. The group characteristically takes control over the society, whether by seizing government power or by constant harassment of a public. The number of points on which the elite group can enforce conformity is very limited. Hence the fundamentalist tenets will of their nature be extremely reductionist, reducing religious practice to a few gross externals.

The most important thing to know about it is that the fundamentalist phenomenon has nothing whatever to do with religious faith. It is exclusively about power, the enforcement of an inner elite's authority over a society. As such, it is dependent upon promoting hysteria, a sense of the whole society's endangerment if it does not conform, of the treasonable character of any dissent, of the need to defend the society against foreign aggressors. It musters religious conformity, basically external, and summary punishment of dissenters, in the name of these objectives. We see this pattern often enough in the much abused Islamic world that the concept of this sort of fundamentalism is frequently identified with angry Islamic militancy. It can be seen as well among angry Indian Hindus burning mosques, among Jewish settlers in the occupied Palestinian territories, intent on driving out the remaining Palestinian population, in the extremes of the American militant Right. In its more moderated forms it shows itself in a less violent political Right, often concentrated still among Protestants on biblical literalism, among Catholic on doctrinal conformity.

In much of this fundamentalist militancy we come across savage and punitive doctrines of God. We hear much interest in our time on whether people "believe in God," some degree of religious commitment understood when a large percentage of people profess such belief, but little questioning, in public, of what people believe of God. Beliefs in God as a frightful visitor of terror upon his world and upon all who offend against his the rule of his chosen coincide with some of the most coercive forms of fundamentalism understood in this sense. It occurs especially among people conscious of deep grievance, who expect a vengeful God to vindicate their cause.

How, in the name of authentic religious faith, do we respond to the rage of these fundamentalist zealots? As Christians we have a central responsibility for the task of reconciliation, hence to counter any such militant extremes. Blessed are the peacemakers. A curious thing happened to the doctrine of reconciliation in the course of Christian history, in that it became privatized, purely a matter between the individual and God. In Catholic practice, reconciliation disappeared into the confessional, where merely individual sins were to be forgiven. In more conservative Protestant theology, too, the expectation of reconciliation tended to be limited to that between God and the individual. Forgiveness between human persons and groups disappeared from the menu, the overarching vision that we would be forgiven as we forgive others forgotten. Far from our consciousness was the fixing of priorities in Matthew 5, 23-24: "If, when you are bringing your gift to the altar, you suddenly remember that your brother has a grievance against you, leave your gift where it is before the altar. First go and make your peace with your brother, and only then come back and offer your gift."

This is a work of all religious faiths, and we neglect at our peril cooperation with the workers for reconciliation of other faiths. We need seriously to assess our resources, and make this a basic theme of the pastoral training for Christian ministry.

Rabbi Marc Gopin, author of the recent *Between Eden and Armageddon: The Future of World Religions, Violence and Peacemaking*, offers one conspicuous approach. Gopin, a frequent visitor and mediator in the Middle Eastern conflict, seeks always to penetrate the actual contemporary religious language of the militant factions, in his case often of the most fundamentalist settler groups, to find deep within their traditional paradigms the stimuli to peacemaking. Much in contrast to this approach, his close colleague Abul Aziz Sachedina, author of *The Islamic Roots of Democratic Pluralism*, seeks to cut through all the accretions of secondary tradition to find in the primary text of the *Koran* itself the basis for recognizing the legitimacy of other faith traditions and validating them and their faith communities. And if we seek a deep exploration of the Christian roots of reconciliation, we can do no better than to consult the work of the Croatian Evangelical theologian Miroslav Volf.

Technical proficiency is of the essence if we are to take seriously the religious and Christian responsibility for peacemaking, justice and the overcoming of violence. Within the United States, the work of Mennonites and the Conflict Transformation Program of Eastern Mennonite University have become a preeminent example of serious Christian endeavor in this sphere. We bring our various talents to the task. A Special Report of the U.S. Institute of Peace points out how generally lacking Catholic institutions have shown themselves in technical expertise, yet how profoundly they have explored the justice premises of genuine reconciliation. It pays special tribute to the outstanding work of the worldwide Sant' Egidio Community, fostering peace and protecting its proponents in such bitter conflicts as those of Mozambique and Kosovo, all this not as a special calling but as a natural dimension of its mission of deepening the spiritual life and faith commitment of its members.

Here in Boston, within the academic consortium of nine Christian institutions of theological study, Protestant, Catholic and Orthodox, the Boston Theological Institute, we have found it incumbent on us to develop awareness of the Christian mission of reconciliation in the concrete circumstances of conflicts in various parts of the world. We have conducted workshop visits by graduate students of theology to regions of conflict–Northern Ireland, the countries of the former Yugoslavia, South Africa, Jerusalem and the Middle East, Cuba–and in the process have prepared original video documentaries about the process of peacemaking and the promotion of social justice in those countries. In the special situation of the Balkan countries, we conducted, in Fenruary of 2000, a conference of theology students from Bosnia, Serbia and Croatia, to help them come to an understanding of one another's role as victims of the wars.

So, what in general can we say of the responsibility of the churches for promotion of reconciliation and the overcoming of violence? A decade dedicated to the purpose is welcome, but after the long neglect of this task in Christian mission it is hardly just one decade's work. Our churches have a long and largely shameful legacy of violent conflict among themselves and of coercive imposition on others, particularly during the epoch of imperial conquest. We have need of penance and the admission of guilt and failure, which in turn should lead us to some humility as we face this long neglected task.

We need to see freshly the centrality of the work of reconciliation and forgiveness, and of a justice that restores rather than destroys relations among all those created in the image of God. We are called to be merciful and compassionate as is our Father in heaven, to feed the hungry, comfort the sorrowing, aid the oppressed, make peace among enemies, to be perfect as our heavenly Father is perfect. That is our mission as church. It is in our work of forgiveness and reconciliation that that perfection will be measured.

## 22.
## The Politics of Globalization: A Matrix for Religious Identity and Conceptions of Citizenship

By Rodney L. Petersen
Boston Theological Institute

The book, *Managing Global Chaos* (Crocker, et al), was given a new twist on September 11. The ways in which issues of macro-economic policy and regional political stability were spun, appeared to give new cogency to Samuel Huntington's often-quoted thesis defined in his *The Clash of Civilizations*. Such turmoil reminds us that "globalization"–the very term that draws our world together – is yet imprecise, and continues to be subject to further analysis.

Whether we conceive globalization in terms of time-space relationships, planetary integration and compression (Comaroff and Comaroff, 1998), or as the "triumph" of neo-liberal economics (Comaroff and Comaroff, 2000, Richard Falk, Thomas Friedman, Geoffrey Garrett, et al), it is most often discussed from the perspective of economic and political disciplines. Francis Wilson (2000) notes the IMF definition of globalization as a "growing economic interdependence, increasing volume and variety of cross-border transactions in goods and services and of international capital flows, and widespread diffusion of technology." In the face of globalization, this structural and economic reality creates a human reality, which, in the manner of Emile Durkheim, contributes to the construction and destruction of local lifeworlds in societies in transition. In other words, the globalizing forces shape the religious discourse, ritual practices, and views on space-time rhythms. Toward this end, it is appropriate to draw upon the resources of hermeneutic philosophy.

*Living with Transitions:* Globalization is also about transitions. In the first place, transitions occur because of new linkages, such as new bilateral negotiations, inter-governmental commissions, international institutions and financial agreements. Nevertheless, transitions are not merely instrumental, or even systematic in nature, since they affect and are affected by personal and communal life-worlds. This often leads to identity crises, and are often associated with xenophobia, domestic violence, crime and communal violence. Transitions might also imply "translocality," meaning experiences and analyses that go beyond 'the local' identity, and which might obliterate the local particularity.

Generally speaking, the global community underwent different stages and levels of globalization. To this extent, transitions, which were occasioned by globalization, have never been a new phenomenon. Because it is still in our near historical memory, we are familiar with the Eurocentric perspective that stands in tension with other civilization paradigms. Social historians such as Barry Chavannes write of the European intervention in the West Indies. Here he describes the transitions brought about in that region, as it was reordered to reflect a new global paradigm of modernity. Enrique Dussel brings sharp criticism to this Eurocentric globalization, drawing us through his research to reflect on Hispanic modernity and Anglo-Germanic modernity. In each case, he presents the Eurocentric paradigm in contrast with a planetary paradigm. Each transition has assumed its own understanding of citizenship and responsibility. Dussel reminds us that the concept one has of modernity, determines the claim to its realization (as in Habermas), or the type of critique one may formulate against it (as in the postmoderns). Dussel, who identifies modernity with a "planetary paradigm", attempts to recoup what is redeemable in modernity, but to halt the practices of domination and exclusion in the world-system.

*Globalization and paradigms of civilization:* Different paradigms of globalization provide different lenses for understanding contemporary experience. Even if one departs from a Eurocentric paradigm, Dussel's alternative of a "planetary paradigm" is not the only option. It might, first, be nuanced in the fashion of Thomas Berry (*Befriending the Earth*), whose "Ecozoic Age" radically contextualizes not only the European experience, but also that of humanity in a larger ecological picture – quite unfriendly to matters of economic justice and human rights. Furthermore, the world of religious experiences offers additional paradigms that make the Eurocentric paradigm more complex than it might appear. For example, Tom Segev notes the influence of British Anglo-Israelitism – that believed that the Jew was the engine of history – as an attitude that tipped policymakers, such as David

Lloyd George, in the direction of favoring Jewish Zionism (*One Palestine, Complete. Jews and Arabs Under the British Mandate*). Lest this be perceived as an immediate threat to Palestinian experience, prophets of the "Return," like Ezekiel (in 37:1-14), were also prophets of social justice (47:21-23). Another example is the way in which Christianity is not easily partnered with Eurocentrism, even if it stays apart from the critique of modernity. Missiologist Andrew Walls writes of an "indigenizing" principle in Christianity, whereby this religion has itself gone through at least six ages and possible "paradigms" or even "civilizations." The Eurocentric is, by no means, the last (*The Missionary Movement in Christian History. Studies in the Transmission of Faith*).

On the other hand, the experiences and eddies of other civilizations continue their paradigms into the present. The most dominant is that of a larger Arab world, and the tension within Islamic identity. This aspect was particularly raised by Fouad Ajami (*The Dream Palace of the Arabs*), and focused on the paralysis in consciousness between modernity – as an imported element–and the world of tradition. Osama bin Laden represents but one aspect of this tortured relationship.

*Citizenship and a crisis in global culture:* Every paradigm of civilization drives a model for citizenship. "Citizen," a word taken from Old French, a person of *la cité*, describes the ways in which responsible life is defined in social context. Augustine's *City of God* presented a model that drew upon Greco-Roman history set in the context of Judaism universalized through a theology of Jesus. A thousand years later Renaissance thinkers and then theologians like John Calvin redefined this model in accord with the civic realities of early modern Europe. Calvin drew upon republican and biblical imagery that offered a critique of idolatry (II Kings 18:3-4), raised up the role of the magistrate (Ex. 18:13-26), and offered a vision for dissent (Daniel). This conception of citizenship was shaped by events from the Kingdom of Poland-Lithuania to England, where it underwent significant revision in the English Civil Wars (Menna Prestwich, *Internationalism Calvinism*), and was deeply affected by the American and French Revolutions. Jean Jacques Rousseau gave further shape to what this meant, even conceiving of himself as *citoyen du monde* (citizen of the world), drawing in the liberal political theory of the Enlightenment in almost the same years as Alexis de Tocqueville gave the idea of citizenship further shape in light of the American experience.

This view of citizenship, while not wholly unitary, was challenged in the mid-twentieth century by Lenin, Mussolini and Hitler insofar as it represented a common adherence to liberal democracy with its multiparty system, respect for law and property, and ideal of peace and stability (Richard Pipes, *Russia Under the Bolshevik Regime*). It is challenged negatively in the opening years of the twentieth century by State terrorism and other forms of violence without humanitarian restraint (Adrian Guelke, *The Age of Terrorism and the International Political System*). Our conception of citizenship is challenged positively by an enlarged perspective on human experience, made possible by globalization. As with religious experience, one is always religious in a particular way but must be so while in relationship with the world of religious experience, so also one is a citizen in a given locality while also being called upon to be a citizen of the world. This is the real message for citizens of the United States that comes home with the experience of September 11.

Citizenship in an era of globalization is shaped by other traditions. This affects our understanding of social responsibility. Faisal Devji writes about this relationship in Muslim experience in, "Imitatio Muhammadi. Khomeini and the Mystery of Citizenship." In this way Devji draws us to what he believes is an important dimension of Islamic protest in the last third of the twentieth century. He writes of the difference between Muhammed and the way in which a "new Muhammed" is conceived in contemporary Islamic social experience, one that stresses structural causality at the expense of individual causality. One is left to wonder about the extent to which life turns on fate or free will, "so that Muslims are robbed of the moral initiative Khomeini would win them from capitalism." Muhammed as model citizen, outside of time, further moves this idea in a legal rather than contingent direction–and Devji draws us to the Ayatollah's justification of the Islamic jurist by allowing him to take the place of the Imams. This implies the ascendancy of law over inspiration or the sustained attempt, now, to implement the new order through *Sharia* rather than through exhortation and individual moral effort.

Just as the Christian tradition finds in its history models of citizenship that point to a tension between "protesting" and "ordering" so does Islam, to borrow an insight from Sheila McDonough (in Tarek Mitri, *Religion, Law and Society*). In the theory of identification and in his conception of "citizen," as laid down by Khomeini and implicit in this argument, it appears that social exigencies have promoted a hermeneutics that results in a particular mode of metaphorical appropriation or identification that yields a particular political agenda, perhaps reminiscent of religious and political debate in sixteenth century Europe (Hans Hut, Thomas Muntzer, Joachim Hoffman, etc.) and in the seventeenth century array of groups defined by continuing social turmoil and debate.

What appears to be at issue here, whether in our reaction to the bombing of WTC and the Pentagon, or in events surrounding the Iranian Revolution, is not only a loss of individual causality, but a loss of history in the face of immanence. The Kingdom is no longer in transition, but is here and the law defines its parameters. This is, indeed, Fukuyama's "end of history." It is in this light that the debate over human rights can become a sterile defense of the status quo as victims become the scapegoats of a new world order and narratives are set and no longer subject to analysis.

In the world of Islam, Abdulaziz Sachedina moves in a different direction (*The Islamic Roots of Democratic Pluralism*). History is kept alive in his perspective of an evolutionary rather than static view of tradition. Of equal importance to this religious argument, a debate that must happen within the Islamic community, is the way in which the non-Muslim world can promote a psychological climate that fosters analysis and dialogue rather than closes it off. This is a point implied by Joseph Montville in conceptions of Track II diplomacy, forms of cross cultural peacemaking that stand along side of official statecraft (Track I diplomacy).

A model for how such discussion can happen is given in the work of Olga Botcharova (*Forgiveness and Reconciliation*, Helmick and Petersen) as she analyzes cycles of victimhood and victimization in various national settings, something we are watching unfold today as those who have been victims in the past struggle with what it means to be perpetrators or reconcilers in the present. And if forgiveness means anything in politics (*An Ethic for Enemies*, Donald Shriver) then perhaps degrees of forgiveness mark the way toward levels of acceptance and offer steps toward the development of meaningful community life (M. Scott Peck, *Creating Community*). Our ability and willingness to work with conflicting narratives of abuse (Herbert Kelman and Donna Hicks) lays out for us the degree to which globalization will contribute to community or foster communal violence. Citizenship in the 21st century requires narratives that can be analyzed because we have come to recognize the fluid nature of civilization in the context of globalization. These narratives require conversation so that we can develop a common vocabulary (Robert Bellah *et al*, *Habits of the Heart*) for citizenship in an age of globalization.

## 23.
# EarthKeeping as a Dimension of Christian Mission: David Livingstone's attitude Towards Life: A Challenge to EarthKeeping Missions

By John Kaoma
*student,* Episcopal Divinity School

Many books have written about David Livingstone. In Zambia and Britain, Livingstone is an icon of missionary work. As Professor Andrew Walls rightly states:

> If any man in the streets – at least, in any British street – were asked at any time in the last century to name a Christian missionary, it is likely that he would name David Livingstone. This might be indeed the only missionary name he could think of. Somehow, Livingstone has come to stand as the representative missionary, the missionary par excellence. Yet he was hardly a missionary. (Andrew Walls, "The Legacy of David Livingstone" *International Bulletin of Missionary Research*, July, 1987,127.

Indeed, Walls assessment is important in understanding Livingstone. He was a missionary par excellence: yet hardly a missionary. This assessment seems to suggest the two faces Livingstone always carried. In any British street, Livingstone stood as representative missionary par excellence. Yet to a Missiologist, he was hardly a missionary.

That the nineteenth century missionary activities have been interpreted from an anthropocentric perspective makes Livingstone not a typical missionary. However, once missions are interpreted from an ecological and environmental perspective, Livingstone could qualify as a missionary. Some early missionaries documented their observations about the natural environment and the socio-political atmosphere of their time. For instance, Livingstone documented some of his findings about the people and their environment in massive proportions. This fact suggests that modern environmental missions and ecotheology have much to learn from such documents.

The growing consciousness of the ecological crisis has affected every sphere of knowledge. Many religions and fields of study have accepted the reality of this crisis. According to Elizabeth Johnson,

> On the brink of the third millennium, a new consciousness is taking hold among persons around the globe, an understanding shaped a unique dialectic: new knowledge of the earth's intricate workings discovered and popularized by contemporary science, in tension with the realization of how human predation is currently spoiling the natural world. [Elizabeth Johnson, "Losing and Finding Creation in Christian Tradition," *Christianity and Ecology*, D.T Hessel, R R. Ruether ed., Cambridge, Harvard University Press, 2000, 3.]

Johnson's observation begs a new consciousness in every field of study, including missions. Indeed, the most extraordinary task missiologists face today is interpreting Christian missions within the contexts of this consciousness. This new consciousness proposes an environmental or ecological mission. Although civilization and commerce and to some extent missionary activities were characterized by domination or "conquest of the other" in the name of development, environmental missionary activities should be characterized by the concept of relatedness to the other. It implies proclaiming the good news that all life is community, "for in Christ all things hold together." (Col 1:17) Here, humanity in its many races, male and female, nonhuman and the cosmos, become the Community of life to which all including Christianity "ought to convert." [Larry Rasmussen, "Global Eco-justice: The Church's Mission in Urban Society," *Christianity and Ecology*, D.T Hessel and R R. Ruether ed., Cambridge, Harvard University Press,2000, 526.] It means accepting our differences as the very knots of our relatedness whereby no one species can claim power over the other. Therefore, environmental mission is centered on liberating life. It seeks to proclaim the message of hope within the context of the environmental crisis that the Creator was in Christ, reconciling the entire creation in Christ (Col 1:20) Among the early missionaries to Southern Africa, Livingstone possibly understood this better, because in his writings, we are informed about animals, insects, plants, women, and men. He provided a detailed account of the social environment of the people and the very world that made them.

Sadly, such information has been left to geographers and botanists as if it has no value to Christian mission and theology. Arguably, his belief in the sacredness of life, his compassion towards animals and his deep love and concern for human life has not received much attention from Christian historians either. For this reason, I will argue that Livingstone understood himself as having a special responsibility to humanity and to the environment. Unlike many other missionaries, who viewed missionary work as encompassing human life alone, Livingstone held an inclusive mission to the biota. While it is clear that some would insist that he was an explorer, others a pioneer colonialist and some an abolitionist, or simply a geographer, I will argue in conclusion that despite his many faces and paradoxes, Livingstone was a Christian missionary whose belief in the 'sacred regard towards life' and his deep love for nature would inform modern environmental and earthkeeping mission.

## 24.
## *REVELATION 18*
## *The New World & The New World Order*

By Allen D. Callahan
*formerly faculty at* Harvard Divinity School

This article was written in preparation for the Gospel Reggae event, "Kingdom Rise, Kingdom Fall," held on Saturday and Sunday, 12-13 April at Harvard Divinity School, Converse Hall of Tremont Temple Baptist Church, and at The Memorial Church, Harvard University. Issues of globalization, Liberation Theology, Black consciousness and Christian theology & confession will be discussed in the context of Caribbean music, lively drumming, and dance performance.

> And I heard a voice saying unto me: Switch on the radio
> And I did switch it on and heard: BABYLON IS FALLEN
> BABYLON THE GREAT IS FALLEN
> And all the transmitters in the world gave the same news
> And the Angel gave me a check drawn on the National City Bank
> And said unto me: Go thou cash this check
> But no bank would for all the banks were bankrupt
> Skyscrapers were as though they had never been
> A million simultaneous fires yet not one firefighter
> Nor a phone to summon an ambulance nor were there any
> ambulances
> Nor was there enough plasma in the world
> To help the injured of a single city
> And I heard another voice from heaven saying:
> Go forth from her my people
> Lest ye be contaminated by the Radiation
> Lest ye be smitten by the Microbes
> By the Anthrax Bomb
> By the Cholera Bomb

By the Diphtheria Bomb
By the Tularemia Bomb
They will behold the great disaster on TV
For the Bomb is fallen on great Babylon
And they will weep and wail for the Beloved City
Pilots will look down from their planes afraid to approach
The ocean liners will stay anchored far away
For fear lest the atomic leprosy should fall on them …
— Ernesto Cardenal, "Apocalypse"

Revelation 18 is a critique in apocalyptic idiom of the political economy of imperial Rome. There is a great cloud of witnesses in the field of New Testament studies who are congenial to this reading of the text. This reading is congenial to a consensus among exegetes in Latin America and the Caribbean. Pablo Richard writes that the Book of Revelation is "indispensable for building a theological, prophetic, and apocalyptic analysis of our present situation." Our present situation is that of globalization. Now, by globalization I have in mind the definition of Saskia Sassen, which delineates the complex of economic and political features attending the wider empowerment of the United States after the fall of the Soviet Union.

Among these features are the global penetration of U.S. popular culture, the new configuration of international governance supported by the United States and its allies, and the unprecedented expansion of the global market economy with technologically sophisticated apparatuses of communication and exchange. "These developments," writes Max Stackhouse, "are rooted in historic trends that seem now to be leading humanity toward the possible creation of a global civilization that will alter every community and tradition." Richard Schweiker describes this new order of things as including "highly differentiated and coordinated financial and credit systems as well as high-tech industries and even postindustrial information flows that are influencing all aspects of economic life." Pablo Richard's reading is emblematic of a broad consensus of Latin American and Caribbean exegetes who are reading Revelation 18 in the shadow of globalization.

In their traditional exegesis, the Rastafarians of Jamaica anticipated the interpretation of the contemporary significance of the Babylon imagery of Revelation for global political economy. The Rastas "do not employ biblical figures allegorically or typologically; that is, they do not use the semiotic stuff of the Bible to represent aspects of historical and contemporary experience." Instead, in Rasta exegesis, Babylon is a comprehensive sign for domination in the Atlantic world, "symbolic of a complex of oppressive forces represented by slavery, colonialism, imperialism and the systems and ideologies that enforce and sustain them and their aftereffects." In the light of this interpretation of Babylon, Rastas have assumed a posture of cultural, economic, and political resistance to the principalities and powers of globalization. The Rastas have effectively translated the imperative in Rev 18:4, "Come out of her, my people," into a boycott of the world system. As early as 1971, a Rasta delegate to the ecumenical symposium on development held in Chaguaramas, Trinidad, delineated the following response to the Babylonian captivity of global capital. "The Rasta does not play a part in keeping up Babylon politics but would take part in the development of a just and true politics (a way of running the country), along that of the holy Bible and any other equal and just way that would benefit the people of the Carribean, Africa and the world."

While some Rastas look forward to total liberation only by being fully repatriated in Africa, others hold to an eschatology realizable in the present when Jah, i.e., God, destroys the global regime that they frequently refer to as "Babylon shitstem (i.e., system)." Divine intervention, however, is attended by the struggle of the righteous against the infernal forces of the "shitstem." Theologian Nathaniel Murrell explains that "Rastas believe that the expected liberation could come in the here and now if everyone joins in restructuring the political system and adopting the Rastafari social, economic, and political agenda."

## 25.
## *When the "Who Am I" Meets the "I Am Who"...*
## *Advice for Young Theologians*

By Barry Corey
*formerly* Academic Dean, Gordon-Conwell Theological Seminary
President, Biola University

An excerpt from Exodus 3 and the burning bush... So here is a thought to ponder: What does it mean when you ask your God, "Who are you?" and he answers, "I AM WHO I AM?" The more you reflect on these words, the more awesome they become. Don't expect me to do them justice.

When we ask God how he got to be who he is, he answers, I AM WHO I AM. In other words, nobody put me here. No one gave me a genetic code. I had no beginning. Nothing defines me. Therefore there is no subjectivity to me. Hence...I AM WHO I AM means that his objective Truth is crucial. This disclosure to Moses of a God who is absolute means that what he was he still is and he's gonna be, the same unchanging Truth revealed to all people of every generation. God then and there proclaimed in his self-disclosure that he is an unshakable, unchangeable, unalterable, absolute, big T Truth God.

It is because of the objective I AM throughout his Word that a vigorous and scholarly pursuit of God's Truth will always be a pillar of this seminary. Yet we have to understand that the desert revelation was more than a definition of title. It was not just for Moses during his intimate calling to *believe* that the I AM exists. This was not merely a moment for Moses' cognitive assent to God's deity, for him to say, "OK, God, you are." The disciple James writes, "You believe that there is one God. Good! Even the demons believe that."

God was saying to Moses of that generation and us of this, "I am not merely a concept to be understood and debated. I am not a thought to be mulled over. But I am the living God and I have revealed myself to you and called you by name. And in return you have to know that I am the 'I am who' of verse 14 and you aren't, and you are the 'who am I' of verse 11 and I'm not." Once you understand the mystery and power of the "I am Who," you will better understand your rightful position as the "Who am I," the words Moses used barefoot before the Lord.

There are 237 theological schools across North America offer the master of divinity degree. One of these Mays many of you will be conferred with that degree. But don't be fooled. This is a degree; it's not a title. You are not the master of divinity. God, the I AM, is! You are not here to master God. God is here to master you.

Nearly five years ago my father died, but one of the most poignant images I remember is whenever he prayed—even by himself—he prayed out loud, a small man with a deep voice who prayed with great earnest. As a young boy as I would stand outside his study at home with my ear pressed against the door and listen to him when on his knees he would cry out to his Lord, saying over and over, "Master, master, master." Friends, Exodus 3 teaches us that position is everything. There is but one master.

Our ministry is God-centered. It's not market-driven, the triviality that characterizes so much of so many. That means where we study and minister and counsel and teach is holy ground, not because we are there, but because God is. And we'd better get used to going barefoot, the position Jesus' disciples took as he washed their feet and taught them about being servants. God has called us to barefoot leadership. Barefoot teaching. Barefoot preaching. Barefoot evangelism. Because when the WHO AM I of Ex. 3:11 meets the I AM WHO of Ex. 3:14, we take off our shoes. Because when the WHO AM I meets the I AM WHO, our rightful position is barefoot.

I would argue that Moses was the perfect candidate for leadership because he asked, "Who am I?" Because he struggled with his own worthiness. He wrestled with his own importance and value, despite his pedigree. As you go to the frontlines of ministry, remember many of you have been entrusted with much more than your father and mother, studying God's Word in such depth and being shaped by some of the best minds in Christendom. But we must be careful in our zeal to do good academic work that we don't forfeit our rightful position of humbling ourselves before an all-holy God and crying out to him with our shoes off our feet, saying "Master, Master, Master." Academics separated from loving God more is tantamount to idolatry.

This means that when you're writing up your Greek vocabulary cards, add one that says "Christ is the Alpha and the Omega, the First and the

Last, the Beginning and the End." When you're pondering theories of social ethics, don't forget the pain and brokenness and suffering of those who need us to be there for them in Jesus' name. When you are thick into the study of soteriology, anchor every thought to the fundamental truth that Jesus saves. When you are debating the intricacies of Christology, cling to your hope that only Christ is Lord. When you are thick into missiological research, remember our mandate to be a part of what God is doing around the world today through the power of his Holy Spirit. And when you're going at it over eschatological nuances, don't lose sight of the fact that one of these days Jesus is gonna break through the clouds of glory and he's gonna banish the evil one to the pit of hell once and for all, and Christ shall reign forever and ever.

In his final sermon at this school, New Testament scholar Scott Hafemann reminded us so poignantly that theology must always lead to doxology. We study God more to praise God more. We are not about winning points in a theological debate. When the "who am I" meets the "I am who" we go barefoot, we don't put on steel-toed boots to kick the heresy out of our brother or the Jesus into our culture. The issue is ultimately not about who is right, it is about who is righteous on the basis of Christ's righteousness credited to us and received by faith.

We can disagree, even sharply disagree. But we must do so with humility and love, respecting one another's opinion. No need for power. Because it is not about our winning an argument, it is about God's glory being revealed through an imperfect you to a world. So we are to be strong in our zeal for Truth, but meek in our position.

We need leaders who will emphasize with love and humility the eternal truths of orthodoxy: Jesus as the only way to salvation, the inerrancy of God's Word, the resurrected Christ and who will hold high the Church. Leaders who are unashamedly resolved to communicate the Truth with compassion and relevance to an increasingly pluralistic society. Leaders who are filled with the Holy Spirit of God, who are broken before him, who pray helplessly, who have a hunger and passion for God's Word and who love his people. And we do this by always keeping our "who am I" story under the authority of his "I am who" glory.

I believe there is a reason that the voice of God spoke to Moses out of the fire and not, say, out of a bowl of soup. And that was for Moses and all who open their lives to the Spirit of God to understand that the nature of God is to draw us to his glory, his purifying power, this biblical theophany when God appeared in a flame to demonstrate his glory and power. God was getting across to Moses that position is everything. It's not just knowing about God. It is about standing before the fire of God to melt, refine and purify you, allowing the fire of God's love to take hold, enkindled in your heart anew. Refusing to allow the fire of God in your soul to be extinguished, even as you develop here the skills and critical thinking for effective ministry.

Called by God to take the Gospel to the ends of the world, we have to experience in our hearts the white-hot fire of God that refines us and purifies us and points us like Moses to his glory. As a seminary community, resolve to come barefoot as the "who am I" before the glorious "I am who I am" and your heart, as John Wesley writes, will be strangely warmed. Remember, God is about unveiling his story of salvation. He is the Truth to which all of creation bends. And you are the "who am I" utterly subject to the holy and absolute "I am who."

This is my name, God told Moses, to be remembered from generation to generation. In his story of salvation God writes each chapter one generation at a time. And this generation he will write the chapter through us, sinners whose love can ne'er forget—as we sang earlier—the wormwood and the gall, so go, spread your trophies at his feet and crown him Lord of all. So breathe on us, breath of God, 'til we are wholly thine, until this earthly part of us, glows with thy fire divine. Amen.

## 26.
## *Refugee Ecclesiology: An Example from Liberia*

By Olu Q. Menjay
*formerly student at* Boston University School of Theology

The world refugee population is escalating each year as various forms of hostilities and violence dominate the global landscape. A countless number of individuals have continued to cross international frontiers to seek safety for their lives threatened by uncivil war, political strives and various forms of human violence and persecutions. In 2001 alone, there was an estimated 14.5 million refugees around the world. About 94 countries around the world were either hosting or producing considerable numbers of people being uprooted (The U.S. Committee for Refugees, *World Refugee Survey 1991*). Commenting on the increasingly complex and ever-changing religious picture of our time, John Paul II writes (*Redemptoris Missio*, no. 32):

> Today we face a religious situation which is extremely varied and changing. Peoples are on the move; social and religious realities which were once clear and well defined are today increasingly complex. We need to only think of certain phenomena such as urbanization, mass migration, the flood of refugees... Religious and social upheaval makes it difficult to apply in practice certain ecclesial distinctions and categories to which we have become accustomed."

The consistent movement of the world people, as eloquently described by John Paul II, provides for a careful reflection on the task and structure of the Christian church.

Unquestionably, Christians are not exempt from this record number of the world refugee population. Millions of the world refugees are Christians (Philip Jenkins, *The Next Christendom: The Coming of Global Christianity.* [New York: Oxford University Press, 2002], 219). Hence, the refugee crisis, especially in Africa, is a serious reality that confronts contemporary Christianity. (See Andre Karmaga, ed., *Problems and Promises of African: Toward and Beyond the Year 2000* [Kenya: All Africa Conferences of Churches, 1991], 35-36). About half of the world refugee population comes from Africa. The churches in Africa have consistently been shaped and influenced by the movement of African Christians from their native land to foreign nations due to living conditions interrupted by war, famine, disease, and political instability.

Since Christians are part of the world refugee populace, it is important to examine how Christians in these undesired, impermanent circumstances exercise their faith of Christianity. How do these Christians continue to live out their faith and sing the Lord's songs in their strange and transitory conditions? How are ecclesial communities formed in transitory situations? What is the nature of refugees' faith, practices and commitment in these unfavorable circumstances? What is the nature of church among refugees?

My preoccupation in this article is to examine a church of the Liberia refugee community in Danané, Côte d'Ivoire. I am convinced that the ecclesial experiences of Liberian Christians living as refugees in Danané, a bordering town in the Côte d'Ivoire, provide refreshing and reflective perspectives for what the church is. As Jean-Marc Ela reminds us, "the church has not exhausted its possibilities of expression" (Jean-Marc Ela, *African Cry*, trans. Robert R. Barr [New York: Orbis Book, 1986], 109).

These refreshing and reflective perspectives spring from the natural dynamism of faith and human struggles of a people uprooted from their permanent residence to impermanent residence. The "refugee church," as referred to in this paper, is an ecclesial community of hope, which is Christo-centric. Moreover, it came into existence to meet the needs of Liberians seeking physical and spiritual refuge. Members of this ecclesial community are survivors of a brutal situation. As survivors, they have been tried and tested. The refugee church, therefore, is not necessarily a younger church as it relates to the people's faith. Instead, it is an ecclesial body that is fashioned with a people who have passed through waters and rivers, but did not drown; they have traveled through fire, but were not consumed (Isaiah 43:2). Before I discuss the nature of this refugee church, I will outline the structure of this article in the following manner: first, I will describe the genesis of the Liberian refugee crisis and the emergence of the refugee church in Danané, Côte d'Ivoire. I will then define what the refugee church is and lastly, provide some relevant images of the refugee church.

### A Backdrop of a Refugee Church: A Liberian Example

On Christmas Eve, December 24, 1989, a group of armed fighters, headed by Charles Taylor (who later became president of Liberia until August 11, 2003) crossed the Liberian border with the Côte d'Ivoire to remove from power the then Liberian president Samuel Doe. As an old African adage goes, "when two elephants fight, the ground suffers." The victims of this civil unrest between forces of Samuel Doe and Charles Taylor (the two elephants) were the whole people of Liberia (on the ground.) The civil war resulted in one of the bloodiest carnivals of internal conflict in recent African history. Children were slaughtered; women and young girls were raped; entire families were murdered; members of the families were permanently missing while homes were plundered and burned; people suffered from starvation; and there were acute threats of water-borne diseases. Liberia, Africa's oldest independent nation, was monumentally ruined and permanently disfigured while its people were brutalized by cruelty, hostility, bloodshed and fear. The civil war in Liberia reiterated the fact that war is an evidence of human defeat, failure and destruction.

Given the endemic state of violence and lack of human security during the civil war, thousands of people in Liberia had to flee in search for safety, shelter, food and a semblance of peace and stability. The U.S. Committee of Refugees reports that in 1991, the total number of Liberians displaced was up to 1.26 million, leaving more than half of the country's population displaced within Liberia or refugees in surrounding African countries. More than 730,000 Liberians fled Liberia for neighboring countries such as Guinea, Côte d'Ivoire, Sierra Leone, Ghana and Nigeria. Also in 1991, the peak of the Liberian refugees' migration, Guinea and the Côte d'Ivoire had the largest contingent of Liberian refugees (U.S. Committee for Refugees, *World Refugee Survey 1991*, 91). I was one of the thousand of Liberians who fled to Côte d'Ivoire for refuge.

In 1990, as the refugee population grew in Danané there was a serious challenge for the Liberian Christians there. The challenge was not only to find a place to sleep but also a place to worship the God, who has been their "Refuge" through their "hell" experiences in Liberia. Given the nature of the Côte d'Ivoire, a Francophone nation, there was no English speaking church in Danané for the refugees to worship in. Thus, the refugees needed their own space to worship God. The urgency to worship God emerged out of the people's deep sense of gratitude and praise, and out of the longing for liberation and spiritual renewal.

In late November 1990, a handful of Liberian ministers who were refugees and members of various Liberian protestant denominations such as Baptist, Methodist, Assembly of God, and Pentecostal decided to start a worshipping community, which they eventually named the Liberian Christian Fellowship (LCF). They desired a community of faith so as to provide support and strength for one another living in exile. These core ministers were mostly graduates and students of the African Bible College in Yekepa, Liberia and the Liberian Baptist Theological Seminary in Paynesville, Liberia. These theological institutions were fully funded and led by protestant mission efforts and missionaries from the United States.

These ministers and several of the refugees started meeting for prayers and worship in the living room of an Ivorian family's home. In spite of denominational differences, which had divided Christians in the Liberia they had left, they worshipped and prayed together. These core ministers were determined not to attach this new worshipping body to any single denomination. In using a quote from Kosuke Koyama, these Christians believed that denominationalism has been "the source and the force for 'tearing apart' and 'rending" (Kosuke Koyama, *Water Buffalo Theology,* Twenty-Fifth Anniversary Edition [New York: Orbis Book, 1999], 143). Instead, their current experience as refugees, and common commitment to Jesus Christ, the One in whom "all things hold together" (Col. 1:17) must be the glue for their gathering.

This gathering grew and attracted Liberian refugees from various walks of life and denominational persuasions. Pressure began to mount on this growing fellowship to associate with a denomination so as to receive financial and humanitarian benefits. Several of the core ministers of LCF were invited to join the initial meeting of the newly established Union Baptist church in Danané. This church was associated and funded mostly by a Southern Baptist International Missions effort and headed by Rev. J. Edwin Lloyd, a Liberian Baptist clergy. In the spirit and commitment of Christian ecumenism, the ministers from the Liberian Christian Fellowship (LCF) declined the invitation to join with the Union Baptist Church.

The refusal to join a denominational body by the LCF leadership was an important statement towards the spirit of ecumenism, *oikumene,* among Liberians in exile, while in a way exposing the unhealthy nature of denominationalism among Liberian Christians. In an interview with Rev. Kormah Dorko, one of the organizing ministers of the LCF, he states, "we recognized that we already had several sensitive and insignificant differences as Liberians. Those differences brought us to where we were [as refugees living in Danané.] We were making a conscious effort to allow our common experience as Christians living in exile to unify us." He goes on to say, "denominational identity at that time was not attractive. We were not Baptists, Methodists, Episcopalians, Catholics and Pentecostals; we were Liberian Christians living in a foreign nation." The LCF was the first Liberian Refugee Church in the Côte d'Ivoire. Overall, as Liberian Christians begin to spread in exile, they started refugee churches throughout various locations in neighboring West African countries.

What was the mode of worship for these Christians in exile? These refugees drew from their previous Liberian Christians traditions as they organized their worship services. For instance, those who had been previously guided by "the book," (i.e. Book of Worship, Book of Common Prayers, Hymnbooks or Order of Worship), did not have access to "the book" in this unusually devastating condition. Instead, they had to rely on memories, and more so, on other denominational traditions that were more extemporaneous during their worship service. Much time during worship was allotted for "testimonies" or time when the worshippers could openly share about their various social, psychological and spiritual experiences. They testified about their hurts and their hope. They testified not because life was good, but because God is good and faithful.

What were examples of these shared experiences? The gathered worshippers shared the experience of hunger, unemployment, sickness, anxiety and human suffering. They came together as broken people seeking divine healing and intervention. The confession: "God is our refuge and strength, a very present help in trouble" (Psalm 46:1), was being enacted. Thus, they were exposed to new perspectives on life and faith in their new living condition as refugees, and as victims of an atrocious civil war.

### What is the Refugee Church?

To define the refugee church, it is important to begin by briefly discussing the living conditions of a refugee. Refugees are not the same as immigrants. The underlying similarity of a refugee and an immigrant involves some level of mobility from a native land to a foreign land for various reasons. Nevertheless, refugees are people mostly in an itinerant condition while immigrants are mostly people who have taken permanent residence in a foreign land. The structure of the refugees' lifestyle is very transitory. In many cases, refugees live in temporary accommodations such as tents and designated areas called refugee camps. Unlike immigrants, refugees do not have the means to work and earn income as they live abroad. Instead, refugees live mostly on humanitarian aid or handouts.

Given the above characteristics of what a refugee is and is not, I will make the point that a refugee church is not the same as an immigrant church. The refugee church is comprised of people in social transition, while the immigrant church is made up of people who are permanently stable socially. Moreover, the people in the refugee church find themselves in the state of waiting. These people are waiting patiently for God's promise (Psalm 37:3-9); they are waiting to reunite with scattered friends and family members; they are waiting to return home. They live, worship and serve in a transitional state.

Since the focus in this work is on the refugee church, let us attempt to define the nature of the refugee church. Basically, the refugee church is born out of several spiritual and human needs. *Firstly, the refugee church is born out of the need for faithful witnesses of Jesus Christ.* An essential premise of their witness was how to remain faithful Christians in their unusually difficult lives. How do they continue to serve God when the fig tree does not blossom, there is not fruit on the vines and there is no herd on the stall (Habakkuk 3:17)? As witnesses, these refugee Christians give their testimony to who Jesus is in their transitory condition. Just as Jesus sent his disciples into the entire world as "witnesses" (Acts 1:8), refugee Christians provide evidence of God's love in the midst of living "in-between." As refugee Christians, they too must "bear witness to what they have seen" (John 3:11).

*Second, the refugee church is born out of the need for hope in the situations that seemed convincingly hopeless.* They were in conditions that were uncertain and bleak. Moreover, they were captives of fears, hurts, persecutions and dangerous memories. Nevertheless, these refugee Christians, in using the words of Zechariah 9:12 were "prisoners of hope." The word "hope" in this context is a steppingstone for a search for a brighter and better future. They would sing in their worship gatherings: "If you believe and I believe and we together pray, the Holy Spirit will come down and Liberia will be saved." Hope for the refugees is faith, which is the substance of things hoped for and the proof of the things that is not seen (Hebrews 11:1) Hope is the diet for survival. As Henri Nouwen writes, "hope is trusting that something will be fulfilled, but fulfilled according to the promises [of God] and not to our wishes" (Henri J. M. Nowwen, "A Spirituality of Waiting," *Weaving* 2, no. 1. [January- February 1987]: 10). These refugee Christians trust that God will make their impermanent condition into a permanent and better state.

Let me insert quickly here that the hope enacted by the refugee church, obviously, is not free from ambiguous experiences. The people have been faithful in the midst of hurts and brokenness. In using Paul's language, the refugee church is a church, which has been troubled on every side, but not distressed; perplexed, but not in despaired; persecuted, but not forsaken, cast down, but not destroyed (2 Corinthians 4:8-9).

Hope, for the refugees, then is a word that bridges "today" to "tomorrow." In other words, hope gives reason for looking forward to a tomorrow. This hope exhibited by the refugee Christian is not built on wishful thinking or pious anticipation. Instead, it is constructed on their relational experience with God. Hebrew 6:19 correctly describes this kind of hope as "a sure and steadfast anchor of the soul." Only God can provide hope. The refugee church's vision is ended on the hope that is constructed on Jesus Christ.

Next, the refugee church was born out of the need for healing for a nation that has been brutally bruised and broken by pain, suffering, hatred and death of love ones. No one needs healing if she or he is not bruised, sick or hurting. Many of the refugees experienced the vicious killing of close relatives, friends, neighbors and others; they experienced all forms of inhumanity to themselves and their fellow human beings. Being affected directly and indirectly by the civil war, which afflicted many people with sufferings, they were in need of healing.

*Finally, the refugee church was born out of the need for community.* There was no known organized Liberian refugee body as the Liberians began to settle in Danané. A sense of community (*communus sensus*) for Liberians was missing. The refugee church did not only provide spiritual services for the refugee community. It provided social as well as political services for the entire Liberian refugee community. The refugee church was a clearinghouse of vital information and news to the community. It aided in finding lodgings for newly arrived refugees as well as orientated them to the area. The refugee church was committed to integration and connectedness among a people who have experienced both physical and psychological brokenness. In addition, individuals of the refugee church community voluntarily provided missionary services such as educational and recreational opportunities for refugee children. In essence, the community's *raison d'etre* lay in the need for renewal within human relationships as well as the relationship with God.

The refugee church, in using Tillich's phrase, was "the Community of the New Being" who rested in Jesus Christ, the Liberator and Sustainer of life (Paul Tillich, *Theology of Culture*, ed. Robert C. Kimball [New York: Oxford University Press, 1964], 212). It was not a church founded upon hierarchical authority, denominational persuasion and social status. Instead, it was a church comprising of "primarily a group of people who express a new reality by which they have been grasped." This new reality is comprised of the condition of a people who together seek social and spiritual refuge as they lived and worshipped "in-between."

### Re-Imaging of the Church: A Refugee church

The below images of the refugee church are not new. Instead, these are recycled images, which have been used in the classical description of the church. However, I am reusing these "recycled images" to articulate the social and ecclesial experiences of refugees. These recycled images do not provide meaning to the social and spiritual experiences of refugees. Instead, the refugees' situations provide substance to these images.

Firstly, the refugee church was simply a "pilgrim church" or a church in motion. This pilgrim church believed that their current condition as refugees was temporal. Their condition was an "in-between" condition. Whereas it will not be too long, in the near future, so that they can return home and experience a better situation. As Claire Wolfteich writes, the image of the pilgrim "captures the Christian hope that yearns forward. A pilgrim is a seeker, one who searches out a place of connection and transcendence, beyond her ordinary world" (Claire E. Wolfteich, *American Catholics Through the Twentieth Century: Spirituality, Lay Experience and Public Life* [New York: Crossroad, 2001], 146). These Liberians traveled fearfully and reluctantly to a foreign land without any other choice, due to the inhumane realities of war, while on the other hand having a sight beyond their worldly reality. The biblical epitome of the refugee church is that of the wandering people of God, which is popular in the letter of the Hebrews (David Bosch, *Transforming Mission: Paradigm Shifts in Theology of Mission* [New York: Orbis Books, 1991], 373). In the experience of living in a temporary residence, *paroikia*, in a foreign country, the pilgrim church anticipates a future of permanence. The New Testament passage, "For here we have not lasting city, but we are looking for the city that is to come" (Hebrews 13:14 NRSV), describes the church's anticipation for a better and liberating future. Theologically, I will say that this pilgrim church had an eschatological vision: "For [They] he looked forward to the city that has foundations, whose architect and builder is God" (Hebrews 11:10 NRSV). The refugee church was always looking forward to better days ahead.

Secondly, the refugee church exemplifies the image of the Mystical Body of Christ. These refugees believed that the incarnational Christ, Emmanuel, was with them in their sufferings and disappointments of life. In this light, there is hope in the mysterious presence of Christ. The Mystical Body of Christ's image speaks to fact that God is present even in the worst of human conditions. Through the presence and the activities of the Holy Spirit, Christ is transforming their current experience. They believe as they sing: "I know the Lord will make a way someday." They did not know how and when, but they believed that Jesus would change their state of living.

And thirdly, the refugee church portrays an inclusive image of the Body of Christ. As the Body of Christ, the refugee church, in spite of denominational persuasions, gathers in Christian unity or gathers together in diversity to worship God, and nurture each other in love and grace. Pentecostals, Baptists, Episcopalians, Methodists, Roman Catholics, and others worshipped together as they lived in the same refugee and displaced situation. These worshippers were united in worship service due to their shared faith in Jesus Christ as well as their common field of human struggles and need for healing, peace, and liberation in the time of a brutal civil unrest.

## Concluding Remarks

The primary thrust of this article is that the worldwide church must pay keen attention to the nature and task of the refugee church as portrayed in the Liberian example. Refugee ecclesiology reminds the global Christian church community precisely that the church on earth is not permanent, but a temporary symbol with an eschatological vision. Because the Christian church is on a journey, she is positioned in the "interim" between the first and the second comings of Jesus Christ. Identifying the church as "people of God in transit," Andrew Kirk states, "Christians are in transit" because "they have never landed at their final destination of life" (J. Andrew Kirk, *What is Mission?: Theological Exploration* [Minneapolis: Augsburg Fortress Press, 2000], 232). Historically, the Christian church, therefore, stands between Israel and the *parousia*. Like the refugee church, the global Christian church exists in waiting and preparation for the coming of Christ.

The refugee church bears the image of the earthly and the image of the heavenly (1 Corinthians 15:49). In using Paul's language, the refugee church knows and sees only in part (1 Corinthians 13:12). Also, as John writes in one of his letters, "Beloved, we are God's children now; what we will be has not yet been revealed. What we do know is this: when is revealed . . . we will see him as he is" (1 John 2:3 NRSV). Moreover, the refugee church is not the only church that lives, worships, and serves in a temporary situation. Every Christian church on earth finds itself in a temporary residence, which therefore makes every Christian as temporary resident of this world.

Any theology of the church must accept the reality that the church is within an "in-betwixt" situation. The church on earth is not a perma nent church but a pilgrim church witnessing to the love of God and believing in the promise that God will change the unstable to permanent condition. In closing, I will contend that until Christians as well as ecclesial leaders understand this reality of the church as carefully illustrated in the example of the Liberian refugee church in Danané, the church on earth will continue to be derailed in wrong directions apart from the *mission Dei.*

## 27.
# From Azusa to Zulu Nation:
# Africa and the Ecumenical Movement

By Marlon Millner
*formerly student at* Harvard Divinity School

In the fall of 2003, the largest institutional expression of the ecumenical movement in Africa – the All Africa Conference of Churches – celebrated 40 years of existence. The organization reflected upon the recent challenges upon its very existence. In recent years the organization had faced a financial crisis, which had caused AACC to delay its general assembly one year, to fall 2003 instead of 2002. There has also been a leadership crisis, where one general secretary of the organization had to step down, and the World Council of Churches had to provide an interim leader for the period of one year, until a new leader could be accepted. However, the AACC seems to have overcome these challenges, and many others, at least for now. The biggest challenge facing the AACC is the geo-seismic shift in Christianity from the Western world to Africa. Many scholars have talked about Christianity shifting to the non-Western world in the 21st century, in particular, shifting to Africa. But this shift brings other shifts along with it. The upsurge in Christianity in the non-Western world not only presents an ethnic and cultural shift, but a spiritual, doctrinal and liturgical shift as well. The fastest growing expression of Christianity in the non-Western world is that which might be broadly called Pentecostalism. This Pentecostalism involves intense bodily worship, phenomenological engagement with the Bible, and most of all, prominent attention given to the doctrine and experience of the Holy Spirit. At once these points may seem to be in line with African Christianity. However, this writer contends that the institutional structures of ecumenism in Africa are a holdover, a neo-colonial vestige of the Western world. Even as the AACC theorizes on how to become more African-centered in its ecumenical commitment, a grassroots protest against the formal structures of ecumenism has already emerged, not only in Africa, but around the world, in various Pentecostal manifestations. This paper wants to examine the prospects of the central place of Africa in the ecumenical movement in light of these changes.

For the purpose of this paper, it might help fill the terms "ecumenism" and "ecumenical movement" with content. When this paper refers to those two terms, it is referring to the creation of institutional structures in Africa, which are patterned after such institutional structures in Europe and America. These institutional structures are usually, but not exclusively, made up of so-called mainline Protestant churches, such as Reformed, Methodist and Lutheran, in addition to certain Anglican and Orthodox communions. These movements are usually maintained through councils and issues are adjudicated through a conciliar process. Undoubtedly, more forms of ecumenism exist, and may be discussed in this paper, but it is this key idea to which any other understandings of ecumenism will be compared, and against which any alternative modes of ecumenism will be evaluated. That said the formal, institutional ecumenical movement has its roots in Africa from the 1950s. Those beginnings have their origins in the beginnings of the Western norm of ecumenism–the World Council of Churches. And some background on the context of the formation of the WCC is in order. The history of what becomes the World Council of Churches predates World War II. According to the WCC, the roots for their institutional ecumenism date to even the 19th century, but really begin to take on shape in 1920, when the ecumenical Patriarchate of Constantinople became the first church to openly call for a formal ecumenical organization. This message came during the first major conflict of the modern era–World War I, which resulted in the formation of the League of Nations, which ultimately became the United Nations. In fact, the first suggested name for the council was the "League of Churches." Over the next 19 years, there were several meetings and consultations, which evolved into a provisional committee responsible for the formation of the WCC. However, a formal first assembly of the WCC, planned for August 1941 was put on hold because of the escalation of WWII. And while the website does not talk about the specifics of the outbreak of the war and the formation of this institutional ecumenical body, one cannot forget how many churches remained silent during the Jewish holocaust, which took place during the decade of the 1930s and continued until near the end of the war. It was during the war years that leading liberal and ecumenical theologians like Karl Barth and Paul Tillich emerge. Barth becomes known for his neo-orthodoxy, but for also being part of the confessing church in Germany, which refused to give formal allegiance to Hitler and Nazism. However, the actions of Barth, and other theologians, like Tillich, who left Germany, did little, as much of the church in its Orthodox, Protestant and Catholic strains remained silent during this period.

The backdrop of fragmentation of the Western world and the imperial domination of the rest of the world by that Western world is the context in which liberal theology and institutional expressions of ecumenism emerged. African church leaders have noted that when the World Council was formed, there was at least one African church involved – the Ethiopian Orthodox Church. [Note: Samuel Kobia, "Together on the Journey of Hope: The World Council of Churches in Solidarity with African Churches," unpublished speech presented at the 8th general assembly of the All Africa Conference of Churches, (Nov. 24, 2003, Yaounde, Cameroon) 2] However, it would be at least one more decade before the same nature of political crises that birthed the primarily white World Council of Churches would birth the All Africa Conference of Churches. In 1958, in Ibadan, Nigeria, leaders of mainly missionary churches in Africa met to consider forming themselves into an ecumenical body. Some meetings ensued after Ibadan, resulting in a pivotal meeting in Kampala, Uganda in 1963. [Note: Nyambura Njoroge, "Editorial," *Ecumenical Review: the Quarterly of the World Council of Churches* Vol. 53 No. 3 (2001) 293]

> Our fathers and mothers in the faith, following the clarion call of Ibadan in 1958, that the Christian Church must seek to ensure that the new Africa is built on the strong foundation of Christian spirituality, declared that the AACC must lead in a commitment to the renewal of Christian Spirituality and Africanness by moving the African Churches to see the Gospel of Jesus Christ as a way of life rather than a creed to merely be recited. They declared that the AACC must help Africans to make Jesus, and not their denominations, the sole object of their faith, understanding the Church to be the messenger to the world, and in our case, primarily to Africa. [Note: Mvume Dandala, "Reflection by the AACC General Secretary," unpublished speech presented at the 8th general assembly of the All Africa Conference of Churches, (Nov. 24, 2003, Yaounde, Cameroon) 2]

In the case of Africa, the social and political backdrop to the formation of the ecumenical movement was the quest for independence by various African "colonials" that had been divided up at the Geneva Convention of 1884-1885. Just as colonies looked forward to a day when they would realize a new Africa of nations (given that the Organization of African Unity was formed that same year), the churches too, look forward to their independence and their role in crafting that Africa. However, the future ahead of them was not one of change driven by institutional forces or formal ecumenical structures, but rather grassroots evolutions and revolutions that continue to challenge the nature of ecumenism in Africa today.

One of the greatest challenges to ecumenical relations in Africa is the continued financial reliance of African churches on their denominational and ecumenical partners. One of the unspoken topics, which does not get dealt with in the reconfiguration of the ecumenical movement is that the mainline churches, which by and large, helped form the Western world ecumenical movement, have been declining in membership since that time, and their resources have declined as well. The African nations and churches remain financially dependent upon their former colonial or missionary powers, even as they attempt to affirm independence. In 1974 at the Lusaka assembly, the AACC attempted to make a radical shift in deciding to accept no outside funding. [Sam Kobia, "Denominationalism in Africa; The Pitfalls of Institutional Ecumenism," *Ecumenical Review: the Quarterly of the World Council of Churches* Vol. 53 No. 3 (2001) 303] That plan failed. Samuel Kobia, a Kenyan Methodist who is now the first African general secretary of the WCC, said the oil crisis and the lack of local church commitment made the moratorium impossible to enforce. However, reverberations from that failed attempt at financial independence still affect the African ecumenical movement, Bishop Mvume Dandala, the new AACC general secretary, reminded the latest assembly.

> "We cannot walk unaware of the African frustrations that erupted with the Lusaka call for a moratorium on overseas resource assistance that sought to kick-start consciousness for meaningful self-reliance in the African Church and on the continent. It has been said that the frustration of the All Africa Conference of Churches stems from the fact that the vision that was so clearly spelt out by the Kampala Assembly and the successive assemblies, was never seriously aligned to the resource capacities of the African Church. We walk into the new millennium, not free of anxieties of being unable to sustain our visions with adequate resources." [Dandala, "Reflection," 3]

The concern about financial resources is a direct challenge to ecumenism because it fosters closer denominational ties, because churches remain dependent on their parent churches, or in some cases, denominational churches from other developing nations. [Kobia, "Denominationalism," 303.] For example Kobia talks about the British Methodist Church still supporting ... Methodist churches in African nations, or among Presbyterians, support coming from some Korean churches for projects in Africa.] Outgoing general secretary of the WCC, Konrad Raiser, in his address to the 8th general assembly noted that ecumenical relationships and partnerships are multilateral, as opposed to bilateral denominational ties. [Konrad Raiser, "Reconfiguration of the Ecumenical Movement," unpublished speech presented at the 8th general assembly of the All Africa Conference of Churches, (Nov. 24, 2003, Yaounde, Cameroon) 2] Raiser also noted a corollary problem that challenges both the multilateral nature of ecumenism and traditional sources of funding. In Africa, especially, non-governmental organizations have emerged to compete for philanthropic dollars that were once funneled almost primarily through faith-based organizations. While there is the emergence of the faith-based initiative in the United States, there is almost the reverse in places like Africa, where the emergence of non-government and non-church agencies that provide healthcare, education and other social services, means more competition and less money for ecumenical partners in developing nations. He offered no near-term solution to the problems of funding.

> "Important as the erosion of the funding base may be for the different partner organizations, we must avoid the impression of a resource driven process and rather sharpen the profile of an ecumenical movement that is carrier and trustee of a vision." [Raiser, "Reconfiguration," 3]

With no immediate solution to the financial problem in view, the very nature of what constitutes ecumenism, particularly as the church moves toward a non-Western center will have to change.

For many in Africa, as well as many people of color, it seems that black, brown and beige people always attain leadership of certain broad-based organizations right at the time they face financial crisis. While it is beyond the scope of this paper to examine all of the variables that led to Kobia's ascendancy to the general secretary position of the WCC, he himself offers a radically different vision of ecumenism in his tenure, which is just beginning, than the large projects financed by Western mainline churches in the rest of the world, which has happened in the past.

> "The growth of the new church-based social movements, especially in rural Africa, poses major challenges to the extension of ecumenical boundaries in which non-traditional ecclesial structures find a home in the household of God. This will further enhance the re-configuration of ecclesiastical structures in which our engagement with Africa is no longer based on institution to institution interaction, but, rather, on the encounter of people in rural communities of Africa sharing the narrative of their life with the life of those in the Western world and Eastern Europe." [Kobia, "Together," 3]

This shift in the nature of what ecumenism is poses a paradox for Africa, in particular.

On the one hand, the mainline protestant churches have historically configured the ecumenical movement, and those churches are almost exclusively missionary churches in Africa. [See Kobia, "Denominationalism"] However, the real emergence of Christianity in Africa mirrors the institutional development of ecumenism in Africa with a grassroots explosion, which was fueled in part by translating the Bible into indigenous languages. At least this is a central claim of Lamin Sanneh in his recent book on Christianity in Africa. [Lamin Sanneh, *Whose Religion is Christianity? The Gospel Beyond the West* (Grand Rapids: Eerdmans, 2003)] Sanneh suggests that the missionary churches, or mainline churches, by and large failed in their project of bringing Christianity to Africa. Citing statistics, Sanneh says there were 8.7 million Christians in 1900, by 1962, a time when colonialism had all but died in Africa, there were about 60 million Christians, and 145 million Muslims. So how could it be that the number of Christians has quintupled in the last 40 years? It was the indigenization of Christianity in post-colonial Africa that has truly made Christianity an African religion, Sanneh argues.

> "As I said, the facts of the expansion of Christianity are little in dispute. It is their significance that requires explanation. One major factor is how this expansion has taken place *after* colonialism and during the period of national awakening. Perhaps colonialism was an obstacle to the growth of Christianity, so that when colonialism ended it removed a stumbling block. A second factor was the delayed effect of Bible translation into African languages. With vernacular translation went cultural renewal, and that encouraged Africans to view Christianity in a favorable light. A third factor was African agency. African stepped

forward to lead the expansion without the disadvantage of foreign compromise. Young people, especially women, were given a role in the church. Another factor little noticed in the statistics is a theological one: Christian expansion was virtually limited to those societies whose people had preserved the indigenous name for God. That was a surprising discovery, because the general feeling that Christianity was incompatible with indigenous ideas of religion. Yet the apparent congruity between Christianity and the indigenous name for God finds a parallel in the fact of Christian expansion occurring *after* rather than during colonialism. In any case, Africans best responded to Christianity where the indigenous religions were strongest, not weakest, suggesting a degree of indigenous compatibility with the gospel, and an implicit conflict with colonial priorities." [Sanneh, *Whose Religion*, 18]

What are the paradoxes raised by Sanneh's argument, paradoxes that challenge the nature of ecumenical discussion in the context of Christianity in Africa? Well, Sanneh certainly suggests that the Africans have more to do with Christianity being in Africa than anyone else. Moreover, he argues strongly for an indigenization that many of the leaders of AACC believed has not yet been achieved. In a speech at the assembly, Kwesi Dickson, outgoing president of the AACC said

"If the Church in Africa is to be effective, it has [to] be involved in the restoration of the dignity of African Christian worship. I therefore call on the AACC to ensure that every corner of the continent, attention is given to the development of appropriate liturgies by all Christian communities. One outstanding failure is that when we meet like this, we are hardly able to celebrate African Christians faith in Africa with our Africanness. In spite of all the research done regarding indigenisation of the Christian faith, somehow we lack the confidence to transform the worship style of most of our churches to be authentically Christian and African. Let us hope that the next Assembly will be a spectacle of African worship and celebration at its best." [Kwesi Dickson, "Report of the AACC President the Most Rev. Prof. Kwesi Dickson," unpublished speech presented at the 8th general assembly of the All Africa Conference of Churches, (Nov. 24, 2003, Yaounde, Cameroon) 11]

There are certainly contradictions of Sanneh's argument in the comments of Dickson. From what angle can we determine who is right, or with whom we should align ourselves? One factor is that it seems that Dickson desires an indigenization that is adjudicated from theological constructions, rather than village worship. For instance, Dickson expresses concerns about the Christian spirituality being expressed across the continent of Africa. [Dickson, "Report," 3] "It is disheartening," he says, "to see our people evidently submitting to materialism, making it take precedence in that brand of spirituality." [Dickson, 4] The brand of spirituality he would seem to be referring to is the brand of spirituality readily manifested in churches of the Pentecostal type, the fastest growing churches in Africa, and around the world.

The Society for Pentecostal Studies recently devoted a full edition of its journal *Pneuma* to the phenomenon of African Pentecostalism. [*Pneuma: The Journal of the Society for Pentecostal Studies* Vol. 24 No. 2 (2002)] In the journal, Ghanaian Pentecostal scholar Kinglsey Larbi argues, like Sanneh, that Christianity is Africa's religion, but Pentecostalism has become one of its primary expressions. [Kingsley Larbi, "African Pentecostalism in the Context of Global Pentecostal Ecumenical Fraternity: Challenges and Opportunities," *Pneuma: The Journal of the Society for Pentecostal Studies* Vol. 24 No. 2 (2002) 138-166] He cites Andrew Walls, who writes, "The characteristic doctrines, liturgy, the ethical codes, the social applications of the faith will increasingly be those prominent in Africa." [Larbi, 138 citing Andrew Walls, "Africa in Christian History: Retrospect and Prospect," *Journal of African Christian Thought* Vol. 1, No. 1 (June 1998) 2] Larbi's mapping of African Pentecostalism closely resembles Sanneh's analysis of Christianity's growth in Africa in general. First, Larbi emphasizes the indigenous emergence of Pentecostalism in Africa. He cites examples of several organizations in various African countries that consider themselves "Pentecostal", but do not trace their origins back to the famous Azusa Street Revival in America, nor to Pentecostal missionaries coming to Africa. In several instances, Larbi argues that Pentecostal missionaries arrived in various African nations only to find the these African initiated churches already practicing what they understood to be speaking in tongues, faith healing and prophecy. [Larbi, 140-142.] For Larbi, this is understood as the first wave of Pentecostalism, from about 1910 through the 1960s. The 1970s and 1980s represent a second wave of growth, fueled primarily by the emergence of various student (college and secondary school) Christian evangelism organizations, again coinciding with the emphasis on growth tied to young people by Sanneh. [Larbi, 142-145] One thing Larbi does that goes against the grain of scholarship by Sanneh and many other scholars of Pentecostal-type churches in Africa, is that he attempts, wrongly I believe, to separate churches in Africa into terms like classical Pentecostal, neo-Pentecostal as distinct from African Initiated

Churches, or AICs. Larbi's argument is that churches that he describes as
"classical Pentecostal" reject AICs as legitimate churches. Moreover, classical
and neo-Pentecostals are Biblical literalists, Evangelical and believe in the
doctrine of initial evidence — that is the sign that a person has experienced
what Pentecostals call the baptism (or indwelling) of the Holy Spirit is that
they will speak in an unknown language. [Larbi, 145-151]

A few things can be said about his attempts at drawing hard lines.
The postmodern condition render attempts at essentializing as problematic
and the definitions tend to say more about the person giving them, that the
people being defined. Larbi obviously wants Pentecostals to be respected
as legitimate Christians, which many AIC churches are not. Ironically, the
AACC is wrestling with how to recognize many AICs because of their
beliefs and practices. It should be noted that some AICs–like Nigeria's
Church of the Aladura–are members of the AACC, but other groups, like
the Kimbanguists, are not. Moreover, some African churches, whether
called AICs or Pentecostal, which have migrated to Europe join ecumenical
organizations, not such much out of a concern for ecumenism, as out of a
concern for legitimacy and respectability. [Note the lecture given the last day
of class by Afe Adogame, one of the visiting fellows at the Harvard Divinity
School Center for the Study of World Religion. Adogame has focused on
churches, like the Celestial Church of Christ, a Nigerian church, which is
growing in Germany, and has sought membership in ecumenical councils
as a way to legitimize its status as a church, although their members engage
in practices like polygamy, that Larbi would argue disqualify them to be
considered Pentecostal.] However, both Larbi and the AACC are missing a
crucial opportunity to embrace Pentecostalism as an African expression of
Christianity. For Larbi, despite his claims of indigenous origin, he works too
hard to harmonize African Pentecostalism with American understandings
of classical Pentecostalism and Evangelicalism to arrive at a position of
respectability. In the case of the AACC, they may have been too influenced
by an ecumenism driven by theological discussions and conciliar statements,
than by the worship practices and beliefs being practiced by the millions of
Africans actually not represented by any church in their ecumenical body.

All the evidence suggests that Christianity's center is moving away
from the West and towards the two-thirds world, in particular Africa. This
movement is reflected in the changing structure of ecumenism. A Kenyan
Methodist is now the general secretary of the World Council of Churches,
and Africans are now general secretaries of the World Alliance of Reformed

Churches, and World Lutheran Federation. However, neither are Reformed or Lutheran expressions of Christianity dominant or growing in Africa. Despite Larbi's attempt to talk about Pentecostalism in Africa as growing indigenously, he harmonizes African Pentecostalism with Western norms of doctrine (Evangelicalism). It's unfortunate that both Africans who are theologically conservative and liberal cannot see Sanneh's greater point, a point echoed by many scholars. Sanneh argues that Christianity is uniquely translatable, and theologians like Harvey Cox and Allan Anderson argue that Pentecostalism pneumatologically adapts to almost every culture where it is found, so as to be one of the most indigenous expressions of spiritual and religious vitality in the world, even as Christianity continues to decline in the West. The challenge is how to move from narrative expressions of faith, as Kobia proposes, to newer, innovative expressions of institutional ecumenism with the shift in theological and cultural commitments? Perhaps the way forward, in what Raiser has called a reconfiguring, will be beyond labels of liberal left or religious right. Larbi, despite his conservative theology, does not want African Pentecostalism captured by conservative American politics. He argues

> The current situation lends itself to the establishment of international alliances and networks between African Pentecostal movements and their Western counterparts. This mutual exchange between multiple centers of influence and varieties of gifts should be based on partnership and equality... [Larbi, 139-140]

This new configuration is already showing signs of life. In the United States, black Pentecostals, like Bishop Charles Blake of the Church of God in Christ, are leading new movements to get Pentecostals who have sat on the sidelines of the HIV/AIDS Pandemic in Africa involved. Other black American Pentecostals, like Bishop Herbert Daughtry have long standing commitments to Pan-Africanism with groups like the African People's Christian Organization. Likewise, many of the churches studied by Larbi have begun serious mission work in Europe and the United States, proving they do not see themselves as dependent mission fields. The WCC and the AACC formed around shared concerns for evangelism, unity, social justice and mutual cooperation and interdependency. But that ecumenism is out of place, if it only exists among leaders of denominations, denominations that may not account for the vast number of African Christians.

# 28.
## The Challenges of Evangelization in America: Contextual Factors

By Monsignor John B. Kauta
Manhattan College, New York, NY

The theme selected for this Consultation is, "Is North America a Mission Field? What Does the World Church Say?" Both questions are directly related to evangelization, or mission. I have taken upon myself the liberty of representing the voice of Africa and my own observations of the problems facing Christianity in America which I have witnessed over the past twenty years. It is not my role here to condemn the Christian Church in North America, but to outline the problems impacting evangelization/mission. We intend to raise questions in the minds of the listeners, always being well aware of the complexities of religion, politics, and culture in this multi-faceted country.

The Christian Church is by definition a community of those who accept the Good News of Christ Jesus and seek together to build the Kingdom of God, while living within it. Evangelization for Christians is Trinitarian and Ecclesial. Through it, people are in touch with the Trinity, the grace of Jesus, the love of God, and the fellowship of the Holy Spirit.[1] Evangelization is a way of revealing God's saving grace through Jesus and the Holy Spirit.[2] It is a way of proclaiming that Jesus is Prophet and Savior[3]–a proclamation of salvation, truth, and a new morality in Jesus.[4]

---

[1] 2 Corinthians 13:13
[2] Romans 10:14-20
[3] Luke 7:16
[4] Revelation 21:5

For Christians, evangelization–the promotion of the Gospel–attempts to transform cultures and peoples, affecting their personal and collective conscience and activities. Documents such as *Evangelii Nuntiandi*[5] and "Decree on the Missionary Activity of the Church"[6] confirm this concept of evangelization.

Evangelization by word and deed and by example and witness is the objective of Christian Churches in imitation of Christ. The Lord Jesus Himself asked His disciples to proclaim the Gospel, beginning in Jerusalem, Judea, and Samaria, extending to the ends of the earth, baptizing and proclaiming repentance.[7] Their way of living was to be an effective means of transforming the world; they were to be the salt of the earth and the light of the world.[8]

The disciples obeyed their Master. The Acts of the Apostles is filled with the stories of Paul and other missionaries of the early Church being prompted by the Holy Spirit[9] to travel from Palestine to Asia Minor and Europe. In the process, sometimes at the risk of persecution, they planted churches and converted nations and cultures.

The model of the pioneer missionaries was an inspiration throughout the centuries for the Church to become global–a Christendom–with its many cultural and ethnic members contributing to her growth, focusing its attention on Christian expansionism. The Church became a territorial occupant of new lands, always challenging indigenous cultures. It was often customary for people to assume the religion of their leader–*cuius regio, eius religio.* Unfortunately, in the course of history, politics and theological differences fractured, rather than unified, the Church.

Historical manuals, such as those authored by Kenneth Scott Latourette, Andrew F. Walls, and Philip Jenkins, document the success of the Church. As the Church membership and power was decreasing in Europe (referred to as "The North"), it was growing in Africa, Asia, Latin America, and other places ("The South"). Walbert Bühlmann demonstrates how the world

---

[5] *Evangelii Nuntiandi*: 7, 9, 13, 18
[6] "Decree on the Missionary Activity of the Church": 2, 35
[7] Acts 1:8; Matthew 28:19-20; Mark 16:15
[8] Matthew 5:9-16
[9] Acts 1:8

Christian population has shifted over the past 100 years from The North to
The South as a result of evangelization.[10]

| Years | 1900 | 1970 | 1980 | 2000 |
|---|---|---|---|---|
| The North | 85% | 57.4% | 51% | 39.8% |
| The South | 15% | 42.6% | 49% | 60.2% |
| Percentage of Christians | 100% | 100% | 100% | 100% |

Jenkins draws our attention to the shift in the balance of Christians in the
world. By the year 2050 he projects that only one Christian in five will be
non-Latino and white, and that the center of gravity of Christianity will
have shifted firmly to the southern hemisphere. Toby Lester in "Oh, Gods"[11]
interviewed Jenkins and attributes this statement to him:

> We need to take the new Christianity very seriously. It is not just
> Christianity plus drums. If we're not careful, fifty years from now
> we may find a largely secular North defining itself against a largely
> Christian South. This will have its implications.

Regretfully, the approach used by some evangelizers in Third World countries
prior to the 1960s generally merited condemnation. Some of them were
identified with colonialism, as is evident in current literature portraying the
reaction of colonized peoples to Christianity. *Missions on Trial* by Bühlmann
would be interesting reading. Force was used to convert people without any
effort to inculturate the Gospel. They forgot that Jesus became flesh and
dwelt among us and that He came to give us an abundance of life.[12] St. Paul
states that God became one of us to share His plan of salvation.[13] People
such as Matteo Ricci and Roberto de Nobili were criticized as innovators.
The intimate transformation of authentic cultural values of people was not
successful; these values were not integrated into Christianity. There was no
dialogue between the Gentiles and Christians.[14]

The American Christian Church was initially established as a result
of persecution of some Christians and Christian religions in Europe. The
new Christians recognized the need of evangelization in their new land. As a

---

[10]  Bühlmann, *With Eyes to See*: 7
[11]  Lester, *Atlantic Monthly* (February 2002): 45
[12]  John 1:14; 10:10
[13]  1 Timothy 2:4
[14]  Acts 14: 8; 17:22

result, at one time America was considered a Christian country. Is there room for evangelization in America today? Are we still Christian? If so, how do we grow? How do we keep from shrinking, considering, for example, that only 41% of Catholics go to church regularly? Where are the other 59%? We dare presume that every Christian Church in North America senses the change in commitment and practice. If Christianity is to be viable in America, it is essential that evangelization take place in our country. This is no easy task, given the prevailing cultural, political, and religious atmosphere.

It is our intention to address now some of the notable challenges to Christianity and to the proclamation of the Good News in North America.

### 1. Pluralism

America is a melting pot of cultures and religions. With immigration, new religious movements from Africa, Asia, and Latin America have become competitors for the souls of the faithful. From Africa, we cite, for instance, The Celestial Church of Christ based in Nigeria, The International Central Gospel Church (Ghana), and The Zion Christian Church with its South African roots. From Asia hail Buddhism, El Shaddai (Philippines), Hinduism, Jainism, Shintoism, the Unification Church of Reverend Sung Myung Moon, to name but a few. The Brazilian Pentecostal (Universal Church of the Kingdom of God—IURD) and the Mexican Light of the World Church have been imported from Latin America. The proliferation of new religions presents a challenge to mainline Christian Churches.

How does Christianity deal with this confrontation of pluralism of religions? Shall Christianity consider them a threat to its very existence? How does one express the uniqueness of Christianity in relationship to religions which originated in Asia? Some Christian authors have questioned the uniqueness of Christianity and regard it just as any other religion—another path to God. You are familiar with the writings of John Hick and Paul F. Knitter. The Vatican has questioned some Catholic theologians, such as Jacques Dupuis, for their teachings on the relationship between Christianity and non-Christian religions. Recall the 2000 document "Dominus Iesus: On the Unicity and Salvific Universality of Jesus Christ and the Church," issued by the Congregation for the Doctrine of the Faith. What is the correct response to the claim of Christianity of being the only channel of salvation?

Given that we advocate respect for different faiths and recognize that we are all "God's People," a theological and scriptural term of endearment endorsed by the Second Vatican Council, is it possible to justify evangelization of other denominations and religions in the United States of America?

Central to this question is the idea, on the one hand, of knowing the truth, claiming the truth, and wanting to share it with others, and yet, on the other hand, respecting others, especially those who do not want to be evangelized. This poses a quandary for those who wish to embrace evangelization. Theologians and theology students are faced with this challenge.

In his article, "Christ Among the Religions," Avery Dulles discussed the following models vis-a-vis pluralism: *coercion, convergence, pluralism and toleration*.[15] Certainly coercion, which Avery Dulles believes has been predominant throughout history, is untenable. We cannot force people to accept our religion. The Crusades and other religious wars have taught us that bitter lesson.

Is the model of convergence acceptable? Is the religious impulse essentially the same in all peoples? Do all religions agree in essence and differ only superficially? Will Christianity accept plurality, that is, that each religion reflects certain aspects of the Divine and that all religions are partially true but need to be supplemented and counterbalanced by the elements of truth found in each other?

Would Christian tolerance of other religions be misunderstood as a rejection of the uniqueness of Christianity?

There is a need to evangelize members of other non-Christian religions; however, this must be performed with sensitivity to other religions without diminishing the uniqueness of Christianity. A reflection on Karl Rahner's concepts of Anonymous Christianity and the Supernatural Existential might be helpful in acknowledging that God's salvific will cannot be contained by human thought and action, but rather that grace extends to nature and the historical dimensions of human beings.[16]

## 2. Freedom of Religion

A basic tenet of American democracy, contributes to the decline of fervor among Christians. It is a basic Christian principle that all individuals must follow their conscience. This calls us to question, extreme as it may seem, whether evangelization is incompatible with liberty. Of course not. On

---

[15] *America* 186, 3 (2002): 8-15

[16] Rahner, Karl, *Theological Investigations* VI: 390-398

one hand, freedom of religion may appear to limit the actions of evangelizers; on the other hand, it encourages evangelization. Christians must be proactive in their efforts to recruit converts.

### 3. Cultural Values

The increasing cultural secularization in America is related to a change in the American value system which has occurred in the last half century, often undermining the call to the Gospel. Secular values presented by our culture compete directly with the teachings of Christ.

A caveat: Christian ministries and churches are increasingly threatened with a loss of their tax-exempt status if they dare question the changes in our cultural values. What an affront to evangelization! It is necessary to focus our attention on some of the value systems which have affected our country and which may have impacted our boldness in proclaiming the Gospel— evangelization. America indeed is a mission territory.

### A) Wealth

The power and the wealth of America tempts Americans to believe that America is entitled to control the world. When America as a world power exerts its force in the world, however, it can marginalize other cultures and polarize people, setting them at odds with the Christian ideal of American leadership as a humble servant. Issues such as the Iraq War or America's enduring identity as the world superpower conflict with Christian ideals of world peace and are contrary to the democratic ideal, particularly when America perpetuates an "I am right—you are wrong" philosophy.

At this point evangelization is most crucial. Christ claimed that the Spirit of God was on Him and that He was sent to liberate those who were oppressed, etc.[17] The Gospels speak of humble service.[18] Christians should not lord it over others. The image of the child in Isaiah[19] leading a lion by the hand can be a paradigm for evangelizing the American mentality.

### B) Materialism

America's consumer culture and the self-centered habits it breeds have widespread implications for evangelization and the culture as a whole. Our

---

[17] Luke 4:18
[18] Mark 10:35-45
[19] Isaiah11:6

appetite for instant gratification and our quest for happiness without regard for higher pursuits of life and liberty may have contributed to a culture of greed. Everyone is after gold—everyone is chasing the golden ring. Some multi-national corporations seem bent on profits at all cost. Simply said, they erode and debase western culture, and at the same time foster contempt for it in the wider world.[20] Cheap labor, child labor, exploitation, oppression, and classism are some glaring defects of globalization of corporations. Isn't the film "Hotel Rwanda" an example of the consequences of firms in search of money without regard for human life and dignity? Multi-national corporations need to take into consideration a moral measurement of the effect they have on the life and the dignity of all those affected by their decisions, especially the poor and the most vulnerable. Wouldn't the dignity of the human person and his inalienable rights be raised if business executives were to change their focus from the bottom line and their golden parachutes to ones which include the welfare of others?

The Gospels are all about sharing and giving.[21] Today, as a result of materialism, the gap between the rich and the poor is ever widening. Here again, we see a polarity between peoples within our society, with some individuals becoming full of themselves and judging others by a material standard, forgetting the story of Dives (the Rich Man) and Lazarus.[22] Is America guilty—does it deserve rebuke by the prophet Amos, who condemned his people for indulging in wine and lamb and sleeping on beds made of gold? Religion in the mind of the prophets is taking care of the widows and the orphans.[23] Does America do this fully? Isn't this fertile ground for mission activity?

Does the theology of the "Option for the Poor" resonate the Gospel values? For some, the basis for the justification of the exploitation of the poor is the Sermon on the Mount, which proclaims poverty as a blessing.[24] There is no room for religion as an opiate of the people as Karl Marx once claimed.

---

[20] *Theology Today* 61 (2005): 449
[21] Matthew 25:34-36; Luke 10:29-37
[22] Luke16:19
[23] Isaiah 1:17; Jeremiah 22:3; Ezekiel 22:7
[24] Matthew 5:3

## C) World Debt/Aid

As part of the process of evangelizing American culture, Christians must encourage America to be involved in the reduction of Third World debt, AIDS/HIV, hunger, and poverty. American Christians must reach out in charity and justice to meet the needs of others. It is not only the American Catholic bishops who have called for solidarity between Africa and the United States.[25] The Joint Conference of the German Churches for Development Questions and other Christian leaders, both in America and Europe, continually toot the same horn.

It is overwhelming that, in the year 2004 alone, 2.4 million Africans died of AIDS. To date AIDS has claimed approximately 17 million deaths in Africa. It is inconceivable that there are 13 million orphans in Africa. Forty (40%) percent of the population is estimated to be below the age of 18. America has the largest economy in the world. Can more of its Gross Domestic Product (GDP) be earmarked for the poor of the world?

James Traub in his article "Freedom from Want" indicates that Africa is not receiving enough U.S. aid because–in the words of President Clinton–there is "no effective political constituency."[26] Apparently votes count. We should evangelize votes! Perhaps Christians can awaken a pro-African constituency here in America.

Where is the compassion of Jesus, Who looked at the crowds and had sympathy for them because "they were like sheep without a shepherd."[27] Jesus accompanied and cared for His people. He walked with them. We too must have sympathy and empathy–vital virtues for evangelization and for Christian living. It is said that Thomas Aquinas once stated "*ubi amor, ibi oculus*" –literally, where there is love, there is an eye.

## D) Morality

Abortion, euthanasia, capital punishment, and the marginalization of those in our utilitarian society who are not seen as producers all point to a culture of death. We see this culture justified under such banners as freedom of the individual and quality of life. This so-called freedom is at odds with natural law and the Gospels. The Greeks spoke of The Logos, Reason, as implanted in every human nature. St. Paul speaks of conscience–the law

---

[25] Fall Meeting of American Catholic Bishops, November 14, 2001

[26] *New York Times*, Magazine section, February 13, 2005:11

[27] Mark 6:34; Matthew 9:36

of nature.[28] It seems difficult to convince some people of the concept of natural law.

Ramon Sampedro received an Oscar nomination for his role in the best foreign film. "Mar Adentro" (The Sea Inside) depicts and defends a quadriplegic struggling to be granted the right to end his life. In the film "Million Dollar Baby," when Hillary Swank became injured and was paralyzed from the neck down, Clint Eastwood acceded to her wishes to end her life. Contrary to the Gospel message, portions of our society accept killing as a means of solving a problem–capital punishment, euthanasia, abortion.

Iain Torrance, in "More Than Regent's Park?," alludes to a group of students at Harvard University listening to James Wilson lecturing on courage during the Holocaust years. Wilson was amazed to find that there was no consensus among the students that the perpetuators of the Holocaust were guilty of a moral horror. Some students had actually commented, "It all depends on your perspective." Torrance further laments that today reverence, restraint, humility, a sense of limits, and the ability to listen and respond to human distress are virtues not provided by the market.[29] On the contrary, the market encourages moral, legal and ethical relativity.

Cardinal Theodore McCarrick of Washington, D.C., recently declared that commitment to human life and dignity and the pursuit of justice and peace are not competing causes. He affirmed that, even though not all issues have equal moral claims, Christians must preach the Gospel of life in every circumstance to protect those whose lives are in danger of destruction.[30]

### E) Racism

Our society has a double standard for ethnic minorities. America proclaims herself as the land of freedom where there is justice for all; yet her culture seems to permit racism and mistreatment of the masses, a direct challenge to Gospel values and to evangelization. How many Rosa Parkses and Martin Luther King, Jrs., do we need to remind us that African-Americans represent 25% of the nation's poor? Some believe that African-Americans are simply lazy and lack intelligence and, consequently, are responsible for their own situation. Terry Golway, in "Return of the Know-Nothings,"

---

[28] Romans 2:14-16
[29] *Theology Today* 61 (2005):449-450
[30] *Origins* 34, 25 (2004):396-397

poses the hypothesis: Is it possible to debate immigration policies without condemning the values of those who wish to come to America?[31] His article refers to people's attitudes towards Hispanic immigrants in contemporary America. One does not need a microscope to see the conditions in which many of these immigrants live and work. One of the publications by the Boston Theological Institute, *One Faith, Many Cultures*, discusses their plight as victims of consumerism.[32]

Mian Ridge in "The Tablet" described midtown Manhattan as a winter wonderland with sumptuous shops on Fifth Avenue, stunning decorations, and ice skating at Rockefeller Center. He compared that to life on the Upper West Side–another America where the working poor rely on charity to feed their children.[33]

Both African-American and Hispanic immigrants are fleeing mainline Christian Churches and finding havens in newly founded churches where they are provided with hospitality and a warm welcome.

Through evangelization, and this again reinforces America as being a mission land, the Christian Churches have the responsibility of bringing about a change in people's prejudices. If Christianity stands idle, it becomes a social sinner. Rather, it should follow the example of Christ, Who loved all humankind including sinners and tax collectors.[34]

### F) Feminism

Androcentrism, the movement toward gender-neutral language in the Bible, and calls for the ordination of women have helped to fractionalize Christian Churches, prompting those in the debate to reach for political labels such as "right" and "left" to describe their differences. Some Churches allow women to be ordained priests and deacons; others do not on the basis that Jesus did not do so and the fact that the priest is acting "*in persona Christi.*" The "right" and the "left" have an ongoing debate and their representatives keep tugging the issues in one direction or the other. A proliferation of literature on the subject of women and the Church abounds. Women throughout the world have called for full representation in the Church and have become a force to be reckoned with in evangelization and its styles.

---

[31] *America* 190, 11 (2004): 6
[32] Costa, Ruy O., ed., *One Faith, Many Cultures*: 136-144
[33] December 18/25, 2004:6
[34] Luke 15:1-2

Many women theologians are involved in the liberation of women, some of whom include Elizabeth Schussler Fiorenza, Elizabeth Johnson, Sallie McFague, Rosemary Ruether, and Deanna A. Thompson.

Women no longer allow themselves to be regarded as the personification of evil (Eve). They reject the patriarchal society, male dominance, and their being defined in terms of relationships to the men in their lives.

History records that women played a tremendous part in the early Church. How can we forget those women who helped Jesus through their own resources, Mary the Mother of Jesus, Mary Magdalene, Dorcas/Tabitha, Phoebe and Prisca.[35] Women's issues and God-talk in the Church severely affect the proclamation of the Gospel and cause polarity among Christians, thereby affecting ecumenism.

### G) Family

One hundred years ago, personal issues pertaining to family, marriage, and sex were not publicly discussed, with the exception of divorce. The Christian Churches were not faced with the issues of gays and lesbians and same-sex marriages. All these lifestyles have now become subjects for academics, mass media, school/college debates, and theological musings.

Most Christian Churches, and the public at large, are in agreement that there should be no discrimination against homosexuals and bi-sexuals. To some, however, to accept same-sex marriages would be to redefine marriage. It would be a clash with faith and Christian practice, with enormous civil and social implications for all. To these people, marriage is the unique, essential, and fundamental relationship between a man and a woman. Basing their argument on the teachings of Christianity and a reflection on human history, they see marriage as an expression of mutual love between a man and a woman, as well as a means of procreation.

To those who are faithful to the traditions of their Churches, same-sex marriages are condemned. Those who want to contract same-sex marriages consider themselves victims of discrimination when denied the opportunity to marry. Christians in Third World countries are breaking relationships with some of the mainline Christian Churches in Europe and America consequent upon this. Fresh in our memory is the recent conflict in the Episcopal Church when a gay cleric was raised to the dignity of bishop. Fractions, fractions!

---

[35] Luke 8:1-3; Mark 16:1-2; Matthew 28:1; Acts 9:36-43; Romans 16:1-3

Is there, through evangelization, a possible common Christian front in conformity with the Scriptures—the Word of God?

Are our families being destabilized by cohabitation, divorce, and overworked parents? The phenomenon of über mothers—well-intentioned, rushing their children around to soccer and baseball games, swim meets, etc.— often limits the quality time they have available to spend with their children.

Importantly, Christian Churches, theologians, and society at large must address the needs of contemporary families in an effort to build a society in accordance with the Gospel. The Acts of the Apostles depicts the ideal Christian family as one where there is unity and sharing and devotion to God.[36]

How can Christian Churches help to overcome the individualism and disparity which are ravaging our families. If we are to cultivate healthy families, perhaps we could adopt the African philosophy of cooperative living, best exemplified by their proverbs, e.g. : "I am, because we are; we are, because I am." Or the Amharic (Ethiopian) proverb: "When spider webs unite, they can tie up a lion." The Sukuma of Tanzania proverb, "One knee does not bring up a child," is not very different from the clarion call sounded by Hillary Rodham Clinton when she said, "It takes a village to raise a child."[37] Evangelization can be the catalyst for the healthy family, the backbone of the healthy society.

*H) Technology*

It is unfortunate that science and religion have at times appeared to be rivals. It is gratifying that the situation is changing for the better. However, subjects such as embryonic and stem-cell research have pitted them against one another. It is not only the Church that wants to set boundaries on these issues: President Bush has endorsed limited embryonic and stem-cell research. According to Gerald Coleman in his article "The Embryonic Stem Cell Research Debate" in "Origins," scientists want politicians to stay out of their petri dishes.[38] It is when scientists take this arbitrary position that religious or faith-based opposition arises. Some Christian Churches are not opposed to technological manipulation produced in a somatic cell nuclear

---

[36] Acts 2:42-47; 4:32-37
[37] Healey, Joseph & Sybertz, Donald, *Towards an African Narrative Theology*: 104-153
[38] *Origins* 34, 23 (2004):364

transfer, e.g., the regeneration of a hand. It is the production of an embryo produced by an ovum fertilized by human sperm in a petri dish and the attempt to clone human beings which raise moral questions.

In the classroom, creationism and evolution, the death of God, and demythologization of the Bible are debated in a way that often causes tension rather than understanding. Instead of the Bible's uniting, people are using it to create division.

Guy Consolmagno in his article "Talking to Techies" helps us to understand that a technical worldview is not always antithetical to religious beliefs.[39] Physical science and biology should, therefore, be a help in our understanding of the world and our own anthropology, as opined by John Polkinghorne:

Yet, in both science and theology, the central question is, and remains, the question of truth. We shall never attain a total grasp of it but in both disciplines we may hope for a developing understanding of it.[40]

*1) Secularization–Politics in America*

It was the intention of the Founding Fathers that the State would not sponsor any religion. The American Constitution guaranteed the freedom of religion, and the Fathers themselves took moral values for granted. The courts through their interpretation of the Constitution have had a strong influence on the increasing separation of Church and State, to the point that today religion is banned in public schools and in the public square. Displays of the Ten Commandments or the Crèche or the Crucifix are similarly prohibited. Politicians have become outspoken in perpetuating a growing split between Church and State, at the same time differentiating between their personal beliefs and public policy. Mario Cuomo's speech at Notre Dame University ("Faith & Government: What Religion Demands & Pluralism Requires") detailed what has become recognized as a classic position. Governor Cuomo explained that he was not comfortable imposing his Catholic beliefs and convictions on others as a government official.[41] During the recent presidential campaign, some Catholic bishops declared sanctions on John Kerry's reception of Communion because of his stance on the issues of abortion, etc. Robert W. McElroy, in his essay "Prudence,

---

[39] *America* 192, 3 (2005):11-13
[40] Polkinghorne, John, *Belief in God in an Age of Science*: 47
[41] *Commonweal* (December 6, 2002):11-12

Politics and the Eucharist," claims that the turbulence surrounding the 2004 presidential election divided both Catholic bishops and the laity.[42]

In "Catholic Politicians: For God or Country," J. Peter Nixon brings to the fore the realization that only Catholic politicians are given a litmus test for their moral values.[43] Isn't it important that all candidates, Democratic or Republican or other, be moral–not just Catholics?

President Bush is considered by some to have been elected because of his stance on moral values. The Evangelicals, formerly a marginalized minority, have become identified as a "moral majority." From being apolitical in the late 1960s, the Evangelicals are now proactive and are calling on all Christians to join them.

In the opinion of Martin Marty, now is the time for us to seek spiritual maturity and create a "convicted civility," thereby drawing upon our convictions to strive to show gentleness and reverence for human life and each other.[44] This helps to define the process of evangelization in America—a mission land.

### 4. Evangelization: Pastoral Ministry/Witness:

In order to effectively transform American culture and society, the Gospel should be proclaimed as a means of liberation—an avenue for resolving the challenges facing the American Christian Churches.

The documents of the Second Vatican Council– "The Decree on the Church's Missionary Activity" and "The Pastoral Constitution on the Church in the Modern World" –challenge Christians to participate in the improvement of the human condition and spirituality. In their quest to apply the light of the Gospel and banish evil, they must write, they must talk, they must inspire, always sensitive to the economic, social, and political dynamics, cognizant that they are the leaven of the world.

Modern theologians, such as Karl Rahner, Walter Kasper, Jürgen Moltmann, and Johannes Metz, exhort Christians to be involved in the public square in response to the command of love of neighbor.[45] For Christians, the love of neighbor demands a commitment at the level of social politics and the courage to criticize our society when love and social justice are lacking.

[42] *America* 192, 3 (2005):8-10

[43] *Commonweal* (February 25, 2005):9-10

[44] Marty, *By Way of Response*: 81

[45] John 13:34-35;15:1-17; Matthew 25:31-46

The Prophets always dared to challenge their times and their peoples, liberating them from circumstances which dehumanized their dignity and relationship with God. Therefore, it is imperative for evangelization in America that there be prophets. These prophetic voices must be the salt and the light of the world—witnesses by word and deed. Jesus enjoined His disciples to be His witnesses in the world.[46]

What better way is there for Christians to reach the un-churched than to extend their hands to them in Christian love? Will the poor not come to us when we care? Will the immigrant run away from us when he knows we are there to protect him? Like Ruth, wherever they go, there we should go.[47] A quote from a Shona (African) proverb is most apropos at this juncture: "Do not scold people on a journey; a foot has no nose."

The responsibility for evangelization of America falls on all Christians, who, according to Peter, are a chosen race, a kingdom of priests, a holy nation.[48]

*5. Lex Credendi; Lex Orandi (the law of faith is the law of prayer):*
The quality of preaching and vibrant liturgies can be a means of satisfying the spiritual hunger of God's people—evangelization. Liturgy, according to the Second Vatican Council, is the summit to which the activity of the Church is directed; at the same time, it is the font from which all her power flows.[49]

Through participation in liturgy, humanity expresses its gratitude to God, acknowledges its guilt, and proclaims and experiences forgiveness. Liturgy assists in overcoming the alienation imposed on individuals by the excessive demands of this world. It places participants in the hands of the Creator/ Greater Transcendental Power. During this sacred time, people are disposed to hear the Word preached and shared.

Why is it that some Christians are attracted to Eastern religions for their spirituality? What is missing in Christian liturgy and spirituality that some Christians are drawn to New Age, esoteric and messianic movements? Is this attraction a result of religious diversity in America or is it a rejection of Judeo/ Christian teachings and lifestyles?

---

[46] Acts 1:8; Luke 24:48
[47] Rt. 1:16
[48] I Peter 2:9
[49] "Constitution on the Sacred Liturgy":10

In this regard, one cannot ignore John Paul II's teaching that liturgical celebrations should become more eloquent signs of Christ's presence in the world.[50]

### 6. Lessons from European Christianity:

Once the cradle of Christendom, now Europe seems to have forsaken its religious and cultural birthrights. What has caused Europe to abandon its patrimony? Whither goes North America? The response or responses to this last question are the basis for this Consultation.

The raison d'etre for this gathering is to provide a forum to share experiences of the present reality of Christianity in North America in the hopes of devising ways to overcome some of its current challenges through the study of Scripture and theology. Basic to this meeting is the desire to engage our society in dialogue in order to build the City of God here on earth in preparation for the future.

Rather than being pessimistic, one must be hopeful, for that is the message of Christianity as elaborated by John Paul II.[51] One should focus on the positive achievements of Christianity, and at the same time be cognizant of Christianity's place in history with all its questions and tribulations. Even though the Book of Revelation promises a new order in God's time,[52] one cannot assume a triumphalistic attitude. It is the role of all Christians to prepare the world for the eventual coming of The Kingdom.

---

[50] "Post-Synodal Apostolic Exhortation *Ecclesia in Europa*" (June 28, 2003):69

[51] "Post-Synodal Apostolic Exhortation *Ecclesia in Europa*" (June 28, 2003)

[52] Revelation 14:15-16; 22:20

## 29.
## *Reduce Child Mortality:*
## *A Public Lecture by Sabina Alekire*

By Jennifer Tessanne
*formerly student at* Episcopal Divinity School

On Thursday, October, 13, 2005, BTI, EDS, and Bread for the World Institute presented the second of a series of Public Forums on Faith and the Millennium Development Goals. The lecture, *Reduce Child Mortality*, was presented by Sabina Alkire, Research Associate at the Global Equity Initiative, Harvard University.

The Millennium Development Goals (MDGs) are tangible milestones on the path to reducing poverty and suffering around the world. These milestones were formulated at the United Nations Millennium Summit in 2000 and were unanimously agreed to by the 189 member states of the United Nations. All member states pledged to achieve these goals by the year 2015. Child mortality reduction addresses the fourth Millennium Development Goal, which is specifically, *to reduce child mortality in the world by two-thirds the mortality rate among children under five by the year 2015.*

Sabina Alkire is an economist, working closely with Amartya Sen (*Valuing Freedoms: Sen's Capability Approach And Poverty Reduction* [Oxford, 2005]). More immediately, she has just co-authored What Can One Person Do? (Church Publishing, 2005). As a person of deep faith (she's also a priest of Church of England), she brings her wisdom and faith to bear upon some of the most complex problems facing our world today. What Can One Person Do?, is an information-packed book that presents a clear picture of poverty today, the goals to reduce poverty as outlined by the Millennium Development Goals, and a practical action list for anyone interested in participating in reducing poverty. This book is a great reference for anyone who missed this lecture.

Inspiring and motivating her audience with vivid word pictures that touch the mind and the heart, Alkire presented a message that was straight-forward, clear, and powerful in its simplicity. Yes, we can make a difference. We honestly can. Her voice echoes the conviction of Jeffrey Sachs, leader of the MDG report *Investing in Development: A Practical Plan to Achieve the Millennium Development Goals.*

> We have the opportunity in the coming decade to cut world poverty by half...practical solutions exist. ... All that is needed is action.

*The Statistics:*

In a summary of information on the fourth MDG, Reducing Child Mortality, Alkire shared the following: Of the 6.4 billion people on earth, 2.2 billion are children. Developing countries are home to 1.9 billion children, where 1 billion people live on less than $2 a day. In these countries almost half the children are at least moderately underweight, a result of inadequate nutrition. Health care systems are fragile at best, and inadequately funded and staffed.

This year, 10.6 million children will die from preventable diseases. Half of the deaths will be in India (2.4 million), Nigeria, China, Pakistan, Ethiopia, and Republic of Congo. Nine of the top ten problem countries are in Africa, with 43 percent of child mortality deaths; South Asia has 33 percent.

These numbers are astounding, considering 70 percent of the deaths are preventable. The information reflects a mortality rate of 97 deaths per 1000 births in some developing countries, as compared to our own U.S. rate of 7 deaths per 1000 births. The Millennium Development Goal is to reduce the mortality rate to approximately 28 deaths per 1000 births.

*Why do they perish?*

Malnutrition is the largest killer of children today, accounting for 60 percent of child deaths; 21 percent die of pneumonia. Other deaths are caused by malaria, measles, diarrhea, and HIV/AIDS. One in five babies dies within the first week of life, usually because of the mother's malnutrition. Forty percent will die within the first month. Seventy percent will never see their first birthday. The solutions to significantly reduce child mortality are "embarrassing in their simplicity", reported Alkire. Two-thirds of these deaths can be prevented by known, low-cost, straightforward interventions. Interventions like vaccinations, antibiotics, and providing education for mothers can make a difference now, even in countries with fragile health systems.

### *What can be done?*

Alkire reminds us that eliminating poverty and its related problems is God's work. In this work we can see God reaching out across the boundaries of church and state and color and race. God is drawing all things into God's self, calling us to take part in this work. We are not in this problem alone. So, what can one person do? We can join hands with the work being done, the work that has been initiated by God, the work that is already going on. Together, we can collaboratively make a difference in the world around us. How can we participate? Alkire suggests the following actions:

1) Pray. Hold people of poverty and their lives in prayer. Use intercessory prayer to bring their pain under the mercy and love of God.

2) Study. That is, lead discussion groups, or participate in book groups, to discuss poverty. Get to know and understand poverty. Help someone else know about it.

3) Financial giving. Think of giving not as the solution, but as an essential part of the response to poverty. Give responsibly, with an eye to international needs.

4) Connect with the impoverished. Participate in a village immersion to broaden your own horizon and better understand the needs of the poor.

5) Advocacy. Write letters to your government representatives, asking them to address the issues of poverty. Alkire also reminds us that change takes time. History tells us that issues, for example suffrage and civil rights in our own country, took many years to accomplish. We are in this for the long haul.

### *Why is it important?*

We live in a time when the solutions to reduce child mortality and poverty are feasible. The problems can be changed by human action. What is lacking is political will. No child is in isolation. Each child is surrounded by family and community. By reducing child mortality, we improve the lives of the children, their family and community, and therefore, the world. As people of faith, let us let God lead us to that end.

# 30.
# *Eradicating Extreme Poverty and Hunger.*
# *Faith and the Millennium Development Goals*

By Fletcher Cox
*formerly student at* Harvard Divinity School

On October 6th 2005, David Beckmann, President of Bread for the World, kicked off a semester-long lecture series that is being held in conjunction with the BTI/EDS course *Global Reconciliation: Faith and the Millennium Development Goals* by addressing political and theological issues that surround the first UN Millennium Development Goal–eradicating extreme poverty and hunger. The target of the first MDG is to reduce by half the number of people who live on less than one dollar per day and the number of people who suffer from hunger by the year 2015. In order for this global goal to be realized within the next ten years, Beckmann asserted that communities of faith need to realize that it is completely feasible to eradicate extreme hunger and poverty in the world, that the key is political activism, and that God is present within the very struggle.

The MDGs serve as a clear message from and to the global community that people do not have to put up with extreme hunger and poverty any longer. A lot of thought and research has gone into these goals, and the procedures and measures for these goals already have been developed. Albeit, the reality of achieving the first MDG is clouded by harsh political and economic realities that exist in developing countries. There is wide agreement that corruption is a serious problem, and that in order for the first MDG to be achieved there must be better governance in developing countries. Furthermore, the achievement of this goal also requires better structures in developed countries that will help to facilitate progress. In order for poverty and hunger to be eradicated, developed countries must accomplish three things. First, it will take more and better development assistance. More funds must be committed to international development and not just to emergency aid. Second, debt cancellation needs to occur. In most developing countries, more money is spent on servicing debts than on public health and education. Third, there needs to be better international trade policy. Farmers in developing countries need to have opportunities to sell their products within the international market. As is, large farm subsidies, especially in the U.S., hinder this process.

Indeed, progress has been made on these issues. In the U.S., for example, there has been a doubling of development assistance to Africa. Some debts are being cancelled, on the order of $50 billion in stocks. Even though Jeffrey Sachs says that the U.S. ought to triple assistance to Africa and Bush says we should double assistance, it is encouraging that there is broad agreement that more needs to be done. The problem lies in the fact that there is always a huge gap between political rhetoric and what actually happens in Congress. Currently, both the Senate and Congress seem to be moving toward decreasing the increases that already have been made.

In light of the disconnection between intention and action, Beckmann held that the key to meeting the first MDG by 2015 is political activism. People of faith need to compliment charity work with work for justice. Within the current political and cultural atmosphere more attention is given to global hunger than to domestic hunger. Global hunger is definitely a crisis, but domestic hunger also must be addressed. Currently, in the U.S., there are 36 million people who live in households that sometimes run out of food. Beckmann asserts that faith communities involved with this problem have bought into a system of direct feeding. While "can" drives and food banks are worthy and worthwhile efforts, direct assistance only accounts for five percent of the value of food that goes to hungry Americans through national nutritional programs. WIC, food stamps and other federal food programs provide the other ninety-five percent. It would cost six to ten billion dollars per year to increase food stamps to a level that would eradicate hunger in the United States. Comparatively, in the U.S., ten billion per week goes toward military expenditures.

With these realities in mind, it becomes very evident that charity work must be accompanied by work for justice. Within this struggle, to win and make a win stick, in terms of legislation, there has to be a bipartisan effort. There must be a movement away from attitudes that are privately generous, yet publicly stingy. This is true on both domestic and international levels. When hardheartedness is institutionalized and publicly defended, political activism can be the key to change laws and structures. Poverty and hunger can be transformed by political decisions.

In theological reflection, Beckmann made five assertions pertaining to the presence of God within the struggle to eradicate extreme poverty and hunger. First of all, God cares deeply about poor and hungry people. Second, the very feasibility of eliminating extreme poverty changes the moral character of poverty. If it is possible, it becomes a moral imperative. Third, Christian witness depends upon solidarity with the poor. The credibility of Christian faith requires practical solidarity with people in need. Next, God is moving within history to liberate poor and hungry people. Correspondingly, God is moving to liberate rich and wealthy people to practical solidarity with the poor. There are miracles to be experienced, but those who are not in the struggle will never witness the miracles. Lastly, the grace of God is manifest in this struggle. The powers that be are cruel to the poor in very specific ways, but there is still joy in the midst of poverty and hunger. God uses people even though people aren't very committed. God can use small steps to make large leaps.

In closing, Beckmann offered three action steps that people can take toward becoming politically active in the effort to achieve the first Millennium Development Goal. People can become part of the *ONE Campaign* to make poverty history (www.one.org). A further step and more intentional step is to join Bread for the World (www.bread.org) in order to receive resources for congressional action. Finally, people can also use the Bread for the World website to write letters to Congress people to voice their opinions about current bills that will cut nutritional aid. Ultimately, the fight to make poverty history requires a wise and sustained effort to promote justice on both domestic and international levels.

# 31.
# *Faith & the Millennium Development Goals*

By Michael Ryan
*formerly student at* Episcopal Divinity School

On Thursday, October 20, 2005, the Rev. Dr. Joan Martin, William W. Rankin Associate Professor of Christian Ethics at the Episcopal Divinity School, spoke on gender equality and the empowerment of women in the context of religious commitments to address global poverty.

The series sponsored by the Boston Theological Institute, the Episcopal Divinity School and Bread for the World Institute features leading economists, policy advocates and academicians speaking on topic "Faith and Millennium Development Goals."

In 2000, UN member states unanimously agreed to implement the Millennium Development Goals (MDGs); eight interrelated strategies the support increased funding and effectiveness of aid assistance, expanded access to education, and the introduction of medical interventions to improve maternal and infant health and stem the spread of deadly disease.

Dr. Martin offered a critique of the challenges facing US leadership on MDG implementation. Citing President Bush's address to the United Nations and related remarks by Secretary of State Condoleezza Rice, Dr. Martin was skeptical that the Administration's disjointed approach to US foreign policy would make it possible for the President to achieve his stated objective of accelerating foreign aid delivery, while undertaking a thoroughgoing assessment designed to refocus US aid policy.

Noting that MDG 3.s first aim is gender equality, as distinct from women's equality, Dr. Martin said, .It is vital that we recognize that gender equality is absolutely essential if we want to achieve outcomes that support sustainable human development." According to Martin, the importance of gender equality was brought into sharp focus during development efforts in the 1990s in Eastern Europe when demographers discovered that there was a rise in rates of suicide, homicide and domestic violence. Martin went on to explain that development experts linked the cause of this spike in violence to a loss of meaningful work and roles for the adult male population in the "New Economy." The theme of human development over economic development was a recurrent theme of the evening's presentation.

Addressing MGD 3's call to empower women, Professor Martin reflected that this, like other MDG goals that seek to support the wellbeing of women offer only a surface level commitment to the work of empowering women. Dr. Martin, while acknowledging that the interventions and metrics proposed for the MDGs have proven successful in narrow economic terms, they fail entirely to address underlying causes and conditions of power imbalances and oppression and will not, therefore, result in true development.

For example the measure used to determine the success or failure of implementing MDG 3 is to *eliminate gender disparity in primary and secondary education, preferably by 2005, and in all levels of education no later than 2015.* Martin notes that while gender parity in education is commendable and worth supporting, it will do nothing to change the underlying cultural, economic and religious forces that are the cause of womens' oppression. Quoting Sri Lankan human rights activist Sunila Abeyesekera, Dr. Martin said, "If we look at the MDGs in terms of women's human rights "and not just women's empowerment." "MDG3 refers to the promotion of equality and the empowerment of women as principles of delivery which should frame the development goals in and of themselves." For Martin, the chief flaw of the MDG framework is its failure to counter the forces of "economic fundamentalism, racism and caste system oppression," the underlying power imbalances that cause global poverty.

On the role of faith, Dr. Martin suggested that church has an opportunity and a responsibility to engage on the MDGs. "Our churches must hold our government's feet to the fire in its commitment to make these goals a reality." She also suggested that the various denominations have a responsibility to educate people about global poverty and involve them in the work of supporting public policies that align with Christian faith commitments.

In closing, Dr. Martin, said that the church "must point yes at these goals, as achievable with political and human will." However she cautioned. "The MDGs are strategic but they are not the ends, because they cannot bring about human liberation, human dignity and human fulfillment which is the Church's vision of human development."

## 32.
# Faith Communities in the Global Partnership for Development with Fr. Raymond G. Helmick

By Bob W. Bell, Jr.
*formerly student at* Harvard Divinity School

O n Thursday, Thursday, December 1, 2005, Raymond G. Helmick, S.J., delivered the lecture "Develop a Global Partnership for Development" at the Episcopal Divinity School. His lecture is the 8th in a series entitled "Faith and the Millennium Development Goals," sponsored by Episcopal Divinity School and the Boston Theological Institute and supported by Bread for the World Institute.

Raymond G. Helmick, S.J., Instructor in Conflict Resolution, Department of Theology, Boston College, has worked extensively in mediation. He has been involved in Northern Ireland since 1972, with the Kurds of Iraq since 1973, with the Lebanese factions since 1982, with Israelis and Palestinians since 1985, with the Kurds of Turkey since 1992, and with the various Balkan countries since 1995. He mediated negotiations between the IRA Army Council and the Northern Ireland Office for six weeks during the hunger strike of 1981. Father Helmick also was invited to the White House for the 1993 signing of the peace accord between Israel and the Palestine Liberation Organization. He joined the Reverend Jesse Jackson in his 1999 mission to Belgrade for the release of three imprisoned American soldiers and the reopening of diplomacy in a tense political situation. He is a founder and executive board member of the U.S. Interreligious Committee for Peace in the Middle East and Senior Associate of the Program in Preventive Diplomacy at the Center for Strategic and International Studies. He is the author and editor of numerous books, monographs, and articles including *Forgiveness and Reconciliation: Religion, Public Policy, and Conflict Transformation* (with Rodney L. Petersen) and *Negotiating Outside the Law: Why Camp David Failed.*

Father Helmick started the discussion by describing Millennium Development Goal (MDG) 8, "Develop a Global Partnership for Development," which he believes is one of the most ambitious MDGs, with its staggering set of targets: developing an open, rule-based, predictable, non-discriminatory trading and financial system; addressing the special needs of the least developed countries, including tariff and quota-free access for least developed countries" exports, an enhanced program of debt relief for heavily indebted poor countries and cancellation of official bilateral debt; addressing particularly the special needs of landlocked developing countries and small island developing States; and dealing comprehensively with the debt problems of developing countries through national and international measures in order to make debt sustainable in the long term. Although MDG 8 and the other 7 MDGs enunciated in the UN program are within the capability of the wealthiest nations of the earth, Father Helmick believes it is highly unlikely that the goals will be fulfilled by 2015 because of such little generosity in actual practice. Although the commitment of the richest nations to devote 0.7% of Gross National Product to Official Development Assistance reaches back thirty-five years ago to 1970, the actual performance has fallen so far short of the proposed target that now the talk is of reaching that level by 2015, rather than accomplishing the program by that time. Of the twenty-two wealthy countries involved, only five of those have yet met or exceeded the 0.7% goal, with the United States registering at the 2nd lowest rate (0.16%) of all countries involved. As a result, accomplishment of the UN's goals is only very modest.

Father Helmick comments that although these goals are not assigned to us, as faith communities, and are surely far beyond any financial means at our disposal, these development goals which promote the welfare of the earth and its peoples are amongst our deepest aspirations. He posed the question, "How can the world's religious bodies help toward these development goals?" For Father Helmick, two responses are required of faith communities: (1) to deal with governments and plead with them to fulfill their commitments; and (2) to talk seriously and respectfully with each other.

Although the organization of the Catholic Church with a central international authority makes possible a united response to critical questions and is useful in other circumstances, Father Helmick prefers the Orthodox ecclesiology of the local church in addressing issues of justice and peace, which brings reflection and decision-making closer to the people and their own practice of faith. In addition to the Catholic Church's Pontifical Council for Justice and Peace, autonomous, non-profit, and non-governmental Catholic peace movements have risen to promote justice and reconciliation, such as Pax Christi International, the Community of St. Egidio, the Focolari, and the Jesuit Refugee Service (JRS), amongst others.

Father Helmick then went on to acknowledge the work of young Jesuit scholars hailing from developing nations, many of whom had served in the Jesuit Refugee Service. Elius Omondi, a young Kenyan Jesuit wrote a splendid paper at Weston Jesuit School of Theology on JRS's need to integrate its aid delivery with programs of sustainable development, advocacy and peace creation in situations marked by protracted conflict. Narcisse Jean-Alcide from Burkino Faso did a seminal study of how the HIV-AIDS crisis in Africa related so closely to the effects of war and poverty that it could not be treated simply as a medical problem but could only be realistically addressed in conjunction with interventions in these social and political areas. Jacques Mutikwele, a young Jesuit from the Republic of Congo, wrote quite insightfully of the war situation in his country and its relation to problems of imperialism, underdevelopment and the failed-state situation during the years of Mobutu's exploitation of the country. Father Helmick brings up their work because a network of these Jesuits now constitutes another resource that all of us concerned with these questions should be aware of. A growing number of these men have now gone on to receive full doctorates in these subjects, have gained valuable experience since then in their fields and are now teaching these disciplines in their own countries.

Returning to the question of how faith communities should contribute to the work of development, Father Helmick insists that we should work to governments but never for them. He concluded with the example of Kenneth Lee, head of the Quaker Peace and Social Witness, with whom he worked while living in London. Kenneth and his Quaker associates developed several programs for Jewish refugee reception and settlement in Britain, told the government that it was their responsibility to continue these programs, and dropped these initiatives into the lap of government with instructions as to how they should be implemented. This paradigm, Father Helmick maintains, is the proper way for faith communities to relate to governments. He ended by saying, "We need to urge them always to fulfill their responsibilities for the development and common good of the world community, but in such a way that we and our own institutions are not compromised by becoming simply arms of government or their propaganda resources. We and our institutions tarnish easily if we let ourselves be identified with the interests of governments."

## 33.
## *Solving the Problem of HIV/AIDS is not as easy as ABC, but ABC helps*

By John C. Bell IV
*formerly student at* Episcopal Divinity School

On Thursday, November 10, 2005, Douglas Huber, whose resume includes countless projects dealing with improving the health of the world's poor, spoke to a group of about 50 on the subject of Combating HIV/AIDS, Malaria and other Diseases at EDS. Dr. Huber's talk was the sixth in a series of ten weekly lectures on the United Nations Millennium Development Goals, often called the MDGs, which lectures are part of a course created by Rodney Peterson and Ian Douglas on the topic of Global Reconciliation. The course explores the ecclesiastical and missiological issues which intertwine with the MDGs. The series is sponsored as a joint effort of EDS, BTI and Bread for the World.

Dr. Huber began with a regret that the United Nation's MDG goal "To begin to reverse the spread of HIV/AIDS by 2015" is merely "to begin" and not a more ambitious goal. An epidemiologist by training with Management Sciences for Health in Boston, Dr. Huber went through a series of measurement indicators that showed both progress and the still-daunting challenge of reducing infectious disease incidence throughout the developing world. He saw some signs of encouragement but these signs are overwhelmed by the statistics indicating the breadth of the pandemic, especially in Africa countries.

Dr. Huber, a member of the BTI community, has spoken widely on the topics of HIV/AIDS, contraception and cultural aspects of disease prevention in India, Africa and many other countries.

Dr. Huber used a power point presentation to highlight figures, prescriptions and policy results. For the audience, the most engaging aspect of his presentation was a segment that addressed the vision put forth in the All African Anglican AIDS Framework in Johannesburg in August 2001: *"We, the Anglican Communion across Africa, pledge ourselves to the promise that future generations will be born and live in a world free from AIDS."* He listed the Framework's key elements relating to prevention beginning with two base statements:

· Sex is a gift from God;

· We are accountable to God and one another for our sexual behavior; we will speak openly about responsible sexual behavior for reducing AIDS transmission. He went on to cite the Framework's focus on the importance of

1. pastoral care
2. counseling
3. HIV care
4. dealing with death and dying
5. providing leadership (including power issues) and
6. education and training

*"It's all about sex, silly!"* read one slide Citing the fact that 90% of AIDS is spread by heterosexual sex, Dr. Huber praised certain African leaders for their early and often unpopular stands on HIV/AIDS. He discussed the tri-legged policy described as A-B-C, which stands for Abstain-Be faithful" use Condoms. To the surprise of many - Dr. Huber asked of the three aspects which did the audience believe most important - the "Be faithful" directive has been most effective. It is, he explained, the policy that is least imbued with conflict. Such conflict appearing not only on a personal level between men and women of various cultures but on an institutional level between forces such as religion and government. In this regard, he cited disagreement over the message that awareness advertising might impart: does the ad promoting the use of condoms (from a country not the US!) showing young people obviously sexually attracted to each other, promote irresponsible sex or does it promote responsible behavior?

Dr. Huber cited Uganda as a country whose efforts to curb HIV/AIDS have been successful. In Uganda the reduction of one type of infection has been astounding. Antenatal AIDS rose from 10 to 35% in five years, then declined, beginning in 1990 when Uganda instituted its anti-AIDS campaign, to below 5% today. Uganda was one of the nations whose president was broadly criticized when he began his anti-AIDS campaign. Many in the

United States may remember that in President Reagan's first term in 1980 he made nearly no mention of the emerging AIDS epidemic and the controversy surrounding Dr. Koop, his Surgeon General, who took a broad, if sometimes seemingly unpredictable view of the US government's proper role in the medical decisions and treatment of the citizenry.

Moving from Uganda to Thailand, Mr. Huber began with the passing of a new law that required all sex workers in brothels to use condoms. Behavioral changes, including marked decrease in the frequency of visits to sex workers and the corresponding drop in HIV prevalence was graphed.

Jim McDonald, Executive VP of Bread for the World and an esteemed guest that night spoke of the empowerment of women that the new Thai law permitted: women can insist on condom use with a vigor and confidence that would not be present or even possible in the absence of the law.

The question of hope: Yes, but not unless we act in answering the question, "Is there hope in parts of Africa?" Dr. Huber cited the McConnachies, South Africa, conference in September 2005. In his description of this program, which aims to deal with currently sick persons, Dr. Huber spoke of the "Companionship in Mission" that is part of the solution. He expanded on the need for the involvement of us individually and the need for us to move institutions to act.

Dr. Huber spoke convincingly of the need to move beyond sending money to include allowing ourselves to be touched, encouraging our churches to consider their own missions and to use "endogenous" interventions as necessary parts of any successful strategy to fight HIV/AIDS. One thought he offered to the audience, which included a number of gifted academics who also are locally active, was perhaps misdirected. "Christians, he said, are good at writing, but less good at doing." "Come and see," suggested Dr. Huber, "go on a pilgrimage."

Dr. Huber finished with a provocative idea that seemed to suggest the that there might be both a physical and spiritual side of what can motivate us to fight and win a war against HIV/AIDS. His final slide read "Formula for Victory? (thought for the day) if sex is a cause, maybe it's also the solution."

## 34.
## Becoming Ambassadors of Hope
## with Dr. Robert Seiple

Jennifer Tessanne
*formerly student at* Episcopal Divinity School

If ever there was an ambassador for hope, it is Dr. Robert Seiple. On December 8, Dr. Seiple spoke at Episcopal Divinity School, participating in one of the final Thursday night lectures presented by Boston Theological Institute, Episcopal Divinity School, and Bread for the World. This lecture series has explored the Millennium Development Goals that were established by the United Nations to reduce poverty worldwide. The lecture was based on his book, *Ambassadors of Hope*, and was designed to help us answer the question, what can one person do in the fight against poverty. Dr. Seiple is a man of hope, an evangelist who has been in the fire of war and poverty and who has worked diligently to do something about it. His latest book is an inspirational "how-to" For anyone interested in the process of faith-based reconciliation. Seiple uses true stories to demonstrate how Christians can be agents of change in our world today. It's a quick read and could easily become *the* handbook for religious leaders, government officials, and anyone interested in helping to heal our broken world.

Dr. Seiple is the former president of World Vision, the largest privately funded relief and development agency in the world. During the Clinton Administration, he served as Ambassador-at-Large for International Religious Freedom. Today he is the founder and chairman of Institute for Global Engagement, a "think tank with legs," created to develop sustainable environments for religious freedom worldwide, and to inspire and equip religious leaders with faith-based methodologies of engagement.

With the meter of well-composed poetry and the tone of an evangelist minister, Dr. Seiple shared his message of hope 'reality' hope. We were first reminded of the quote by George Elliot that describes friendship, the "...comfort of feeling safe with a person neither having to weigh thoughts nor measure words, but pouring them all out, just as they are, chaff and grain together, certain that a faithful hand will take and sift them, keep what is worth keeping, and with a breath of kindness blow the rest away."

From this picturesque moment we are led through some of the realities of today, realities Seiple has witnessed during his work as a Christian peace builder. For example, innocent people are soft targets and are very vulnerable. Innocence goes unprotected. Wars are messy. Civil wars are the worst. Ethnic cleansing is another word for genocide. Diversity is not safe in the world today. Refugees are a strategy of conflict, not a by-product. Categorization of people is the beginning of a downward spiral. It leads to stereotyping. Once a group is stereotyped, it can be demonized, then hated, and then damage and harm can be done to this group.

He shared the story of a woman named Mary, a Christian who almost died for her faith, a woman and whose heart is bigger than any I have ever witnessed. He asked the hard questions, the difficult ones we don't want to think about. What is it about your faith that is worth dying for? Indeed, there are people today who are willing to die for their faith. There are people today who are willing to kill for their religion. We must know what is worth dying for to understand what is worth living for.

In no uncertain terms his message was clear: A superficial faith or a superficial understanding of how one's faith interfaces in the world today has no relevancy.

Seiple answers the question, what can one person do in the fight against poverty, with this: pray, give money, and be more knowledgeable. Understand how to use knowledge to be relevant in the world today. And what should we be knowledgeable about? Seiple offers the Institute of Global Engagement's principles of engagement as his answer. These principles are:

1) Know your faith. Understand it at its deepest and richest best. And know enough about your neighbor's faith to show it respect.

2) Know yourself. Use common sense when engaging the world around us. We are reminded of Jesus' instructions to his disciples as he sent them out, directing them to be gentle as a dove, and shrewd as a snake.

3) Know the real world, and how your faith works in the real world. Our faith can bring consistency to our world. To be effective, we must know about the world around us and how we interact with it.

Armed with this knowledge, we open ourselves to positive opportunities as we engage in the world. We are able to bear witness to the hope that lies within us. And we are better able to bear witness when our hope is grounded in a deep understanding of our faith, the world, and the obstacles that exist as we try to connect the two.

In *Ambassadors for Hope*, Dr. Seiple utilizes a beautiful metaphor for global engagement. He describes a balcony on which spectators are observing those on the dance floor below. The spectators are not involved, but stand apart from the action, from the story unfolding below. It's clean on the balcony, and the spectators are unengaged from the action. On the dance floor, however, the dancers are very engaged. They are moving and emotional and it's messy and sweaty as toes get stepped on and drinks are spilled, and they involve themselves in the dance, that is, in the story of the evening.

In parting, Dr. Seiple shared with us a wish. I now extend it to you. "I hope in your life you have opportunity to become part of the story." May we be engaged with our world, and may our faith be a light of hope for all.

# 35.
## "MY SYSTER'S KEEPER"

By Kathryn House
*formerly student at* Boston University School of Theology

The BTI announced the semester-long series of classes and lectures around the Millennium Development Goals with these words from UN Secretary General Kofi Annan: "We who are strong in love must be remembered as the ones who really did make poverty history." Rev. Dr. Gloria White-Hammond, the final series speaker, certainly lives a life and delivers a message for what it means to be strong in love. No stranger to the BTI, White-Hammond was awarded the 2004 Humanitarian Award for decades of visionary leadership in Boston and most recently for her work in Sudan. She is a pediatrician at the South End Community Health Center and Co-Pastor of Bethel AME Church in Jamaica Plain with her husband Ray. She is also currently serving as co-chair of the Faith in Action Committee for the United Way in Massachusetts.

Returned from Sudan only the night before, White-Hammond addressed the question of "What Can One Person Do?" She began her personal and moving account of work there with scripture from Isaiah 58:9-12, in which true worship is described as work to end oppression and hunger, as well as to rebuild and repair communities. After citing the gruesome details of rape and mutilation which are becoming commonplace in the civil war-turned-genocide now happening in Sudan, she posed a question she has been asking and answering: "Who will be my sister's keeper?"

Dr. White-Hammond offered a brief overview of the complex history of the Sudanese civil war and now genocide at the hands of the "janjaweed" militia group. While several peace agreements have been posed in recent years, estimates place the death toll at 400,000 in the Darfur region alone since 2003. Another tragedy of the genocide has been the thousands of individuals sold into slavery. Dr. White-Hammond became involved with the American anti-slavery group Christian Solidarity International, that partnered with locals to find and then abduct or buy back loved ones from slavery.

Such work has been controversial; critics believe outside intervention has begun to fuel a separate economy. Dr. White-Hammond has chosen to continue her abolition efforts, taking seriously the response of a freed slave: "Tell your people I say 'thank you.'" In 2002, she was one of an eclectic group of 6 women who co-founded My Sister's Keeper, which partners with Sudanese women to work in their communities. Their work thus far has centered around three projects. HIV/AIDS work, securing grinding mills for women that reduce the labor-intensive daily 6-hour task to 30 minutes, and the opening of a girls' school in Gogrial County.

Now in its 3rd year, enrollment at My Sister's Keeper School for Girls is 500 students, with an eventual 1,000 students anticipated. "The most rapid way to bring up an economy is to bring up its girls," Dr. White-Hammond remarked, showing pictures of young girls crowded around mud-hut school rooms. Her observation was reminiscent of other series speakers and a truth certainly embodied in the MDG's. Responding to concerns from major stakeholders including parents and community leaders, the co-founders decided a separate school for girls would be best, where they might be emboldened participants. The school has also addressed the concern for students' safety and proper nutrition, as many were making the 3- hour trek to school in the darkness of the early morning and late evening, often without food, by providing making opportunities available for boarders. Waiving the cost of school fees is also an incentive for parents who could not otherwise afford to educate their girls.

Dr. White-Hammond is clear that she believes the Sudanese conflict is genocide. She pointed to the 1948 UN Convention on Genocide, an attempt to promise .never again. in the wake of the Holocaust, and to Colin Powell's affirmation of the situation in 1994. Her evidence is first-hand as well. During one visit, she and other women collected the stories of 60 women in different refugee camps. Nearly 40% of those women reported being gang raped and mutilated, with scars to which her medical training could attest. In her own words, she "knows for sure" that rape, which can eliminate girls and generations of communities to come, is an instrument of war.

The world must not sit by silently while such violence and abuse against women is allowed to continue. In communities where victims of rape were once ostracized completely, rape is now too common for some of the traditional exclusionary practices. Formerly enslaved women are being viewed as victims and are received back into their communities. Already meager budgets are stretched to add one more chair around the table, and when food assistance is offered, there is an unspoken rule that those who have been recently freed are first. Indeed, a neighbor, to say nothing of a family, can be taken to court for not offering assistance.

The generosity of such communities already setting a challenging example, Dr. White-Hammond then encouraged the audience to take action. How might one person respond to the crisis in Sudan? She advised the audience to stay educated and to speak out, literally, to their national and local representatives, as well as to UN Secretary General Kofi Annan. She eluded to the recently launched "Million Voices for Darfur Campaign," which aims to present President Bush with one million hand-written and electronically posted messages concerning Darfur at a scheduled April 30th meeting. Dr. White-Hammond entreated the audience to respond with immediate action with the words from the Rev. Dr. Martin Luther King, .Procrastination is still the thief of time. Over the bleached bones and jumbled residue of numerous civilizations are written the pathetic words: "Too late." The BTI/Bread for the World lecture series has provided our academic community with much upon which to reflect in regards to the Millennium Development Goals. There are hopes that such a rich experience might prove an influence so that, as a community of one person with one person with one person, we might act with conscience and with haste.

• Call the White House: 202-456-1414; demand that civilian protection be the focus, specifically under the auspices of the already-present African Union.

• Urge local representatives to support HR 3127/ SR1462, the Darfur Peace and Accountability Act of 2005.

• Write your own message . http://www.millionvoicesfordarfur.org/

# 36.
# Orthodoxy:
## Continuing Testimony into a Third Millennium

By Lawrence A. Whitney, LC
Boston University School of Theology

Through the Spring term, the Mission course TM854, "The Shifting Contours of Contemporary Ecumenism: Christian Identity and Mission in the 21st Century," has been running a public lecture series on "Bridging Worlds: Ecumenical and Interfaith Conversation About Mission across the Public Square." The series, from 4-5pm at Boston University School of Theology, Room 325, has welcomed some of the outstanding faculty in our midst to share thoughts on the nature of Christian mission in light of contemporary issues in civil society and in terms of inter-faith and ecumenical realities.

In February, Assistant Professor of Social Ethics, Timothy Patitsas of Holy Cross Greek Orthodox School of Theology, share thoughts on Orthodox Christianity in the 21st century. Dr. Patitsas framed his presentation of Orthodoxy with the image of the church as hospital, seeking to heal the image of God in each person from the distortions of haste, delay, greed, lust, fear, hatred, enmity, etc. The saints, central to Orthodox Christian practice, are images of humanity in fullness or the state of humanity approximating the image of God. Thus, the missional understanding of the church in Orthodoxy is encapsulated in the mission of healing, especially in terms of the five divisions delineated by St. Maximus the Confessor: division between the sexes, division between paradise and the inhabited earth, division between heaven and earth, division between the intelligible and the inexpressible, and division between God and creation. This mission of healing, which Dr. Patitsis identified with reconciliation, is carried out by the church as it bears the cross of Christ. The priestly function, in Orthodoxy, is to stand as the image of Christ bearing the burdens of others. From a Sacramental perspective, Orthodoxy contributes to the mission of reconciliation by inviting the world to the baptismal font of healing.

Dr. Patitsis acknowledged a lack of understanding of the intrinsic meaning of other denominations in Western Orthodoxy resulting from a loss of theological self-awareness in the Orthodox community. And yet, he also pointed out that Orthodoxy has a mission and responsibility to contribute to the unity of the Christian church, which he identified closely with the Pentecostal vision (the vision that took place at Pentecost) of the Spirit of peace. He presented Orthodoxy as having something to contribute to reconciling the kingly vision of Rome with the prophetic vision of Luther, especially as faith and works are reconciled in the Orthodox conception of liturgy. This contribution to church unity is rooted in the Orthodox conception not that it has final truth, but that the true Church is Orthodox in doctrine and life. Thus, there is an inherent uncertainty (or at least qualification through humility) as to whether or not the Orthodox Church is truly Orthodox.

Orthodoxy brings many concepts helpful for the task of reconciliation of forms of Christianity: In the task of reconciling the nominal and the real in western philosophy by experience of uncreated light seen by eyes; in the task of reconciling cross and resurrection through joyful sorrow; the cross is in the resurrection and the resurrection is in the cross; in the task of reconciling anthropology through the category of hypostasis: union of nature and will; in the task of reconciling mind and heart through *noetic* prayer and unknowing; in the task of reconciling heaven and earth in divinization and the immediate presence of the kingdom of God. Through these ideas and qualities, Orthodoxy brings both witness and humility to the ecumenical and interfaith table of dialogue.

## 37.
## *What Can One Person Do?*
## *The Liturgy After the Liturgy*

By Rodney L. Petersen
Boston Theological Institute

Orthodox theologian Ion Bria pioneered the term, "the liturgy after the liturgy." In this Easter (and Passover) period we might think, "What is our liturgy after the liturgy?" And here, few books can match *What Can One Person Do? Faith to Heal a Broken World,* by Sabina Alkire and Edmund Newell with Ann Barham, Chloe Breyer, and Ian T. Douglas. New York: Church Publishing, 2005.

The thrust of this collaborative work, growing out of an Anglican and Episcopal context, is that one person can make a difference. Writing from a perspective that is larger than this communion or its divisions, Sabina Alkire, economist and Anglican priest, Edmund Newell, Canon Chancellor of St. Paul.s Cathedral, London, and their collaborators call us to craft a mission for the human community that combats hunger and promotes human flourishing.

*What Can One Person Do?* seeks to marshal the energy of those concerned about global poverty and hunger. This energy, aim and vision are linked to the Millennium Development Goals, the eight goals unanimously agreed to by the 189 member states of the United Nations at the Millennium Summit in 2000 that commits the international community to an expanded vision of international development that promotes global social and economic justice by 2015. These goals are to: 1) eradicate extreme poverty and hunger, 2) achieve universal primary education, 3) promote gender equality and empower women, 4) reduce child mortality, 5) improve maternal health, 6) combat HIV/AIDS, malaria and other diseases, 7) ensure environmental sustainability, and 8) develop a global partnership for development. The

Millennium Development Goals (MDGs) are tangible milestones on the path to reducing poverty and suffering around the world.

The eight chapters that frame these goals are punctuated by study questions and "Action Steps." The first chapter, "Beyond a Dollar a Day. What are the MDGs?" identifies the MDGs by reminding us that most of the world lives on less than the equivalent of US $1 a day. Of the 6.4 billion people on earth, 2.2 billion are children. Malnutrition is the largest killer of children today, accounting for 60 percent of child deaths; 21 percent die of pneumonia. Other deaths are caused by malaria, measles, diarrhea, and HIV/AIDS. One in five babies dies within the first week of life, usually because of the mother's malnutrition. Forty percent will die within the first month. Seventy percent will never see their first birthday. The solutions to significantly reduce child mortality are "embarrassing in their simplicity," reports Alkire, and can be prevented by known, low-cost, straight-forward interventions. The chapter closes with the first "Action Step": Prayer–and prayers and questions are offered that are appropriate for individual or group reflection.

EDS Professor Ian Douglas writes the second chapter, "The Mission of God." The chapter probes the question of how we live in light of global poverty and its manifest complications. Through a brief survey of Christian mission, Douglas takes us to a perspective that offers the MDGs as the appropriate shape of a contemporary mission dei, God's mission as viewed through an integrated understanding of scripture. Again, the Action Step: Study. This time the questions directed to probe our understanding of mission and engagement with it or lack thereof.

Chapter 3, "'When Did We See You?' Justice and Judgment," opens with U2's Bono, writing that Rock Stars can help to shape global consciousness. They can help to awaken us out of our indifference. Juxtaposed with Bono is Liberation Theologian Gustavo Gutierrez: "love of God is unavoidably expressed through love of one's neighbor" (63); and citing C. E. B. Cranfield, the "Real Presence of the Risen Christ" in the poor and marginalized. The point is driven home by study questions and a next Action Step that underscores stewardship: *Join the One Campaign with its encouragement to give 0.7 percent of one's income to alleviate global hunger.*

In Chapter 4, "Who Are the Poor?" we encounter some of the formative thinking behind this book insofar as it is connected with Alkire, a vision that is consonant with a perspective on development, derivative of Noble Prize recipient Amartya Sen, *Development as Freedom* (Knopf, 1999). Here development is not seen so much in terms of GDP but as "the real freedoms that people enjoy." For Alkire, as in her *Valuing Freedoms: Sen's Capability Approach And Poverty Reduction* (Oxford, 2005), economic development should expand "valuable" freedoms. Alkire's interest is in how we identify what is valuable. Her work has promoted micro-credit as a means to reducing poverty so as to enhance human freedom. Building on previous chapters, the authors contend that a reduction in poverty is a part of the justice God requires of us. Moving us beyond justice to see the "artwork" of God, using the ideas of Oscar Romero our authors seek to promote .liberation from something that enslaves, for something that ennobles us."

Each of the eight chapters begins or makes reference to personal stores, particularly poignant in chapter 5, "Where is God When People Suffer?" Here a story of HIV/AIDS as it intermingles with extreme poverty, and the question: *"How can there be a God of love when there is so much suffering in the world?"* MDG 6: "Combat HIV/AIDS, malaria, and other diseases" is set in the context of traditional themes as suffering and soul-making are juxtaposed: free will, the omnipotence of God, Jesus Christ as God.s entrance into suffering, but also suffering and the absence of God, i.e., Golgotha. And here the "Action Step" is liturgy.

Chapter 6, "The Body of Christ" opens with: "What can one person do? As much or as little as one wants to do." The example of Archbishop Oscar Romero is offered up as an answer and a program: worship and struggle against the social problems we face. The analogy of the people of God as the body of Christ (I Corinthians 12) is the operative model. As previous chapters focused on the moral and spiritual imperative for Christians to be involved in poverty reduction, this chapter focuses on the possibility–as judged by those outside the church "that Christians" increased engagement could leave a lasting imprint on global poverty and on the planet. Again, questions follow and here focus leads towards MDG 7: "Ensure environmental sustainability."

Episcopal priest and interfaith coordinator, Chloe Breyer, opens Chapter 7, "On Giants. Shoulders: Stories to Inspire," by reminding us of past achievements of church-based movements, ending the slave trade in the British Empire and an end Apartheid in South Africa. The purpose of the chapter is to encourage with these reminders from the past in the current work of fighting poverty. Chapter 8, "The Spirit of Social Justice," explores the spiritual phases that emerges when poverty reduction becomes a significant priority, phases of engagement: compassion, responsibility, respect, humility, and dependence.

Churches have long been committed to the goals encapsulated by the MDGs. In response to the MDGs the Anglican Archbishop of Cape Town, the Most Reverend Njongonkulu Ndungane, together with the Micah Challenge, launched a global campaign to mobilize millions of Christians in 100 countries to press their governments to halve poverty by the UN's goal of 2015. Last summer in Washington, D.C. on June 7, 2005, religious leaders under the impetus of the National Council of Churches and Bread for the World drew together persons of Jewish, Catholic, Orthodox, Protestant, Muslim, Sikh and Buddhist traditions to urge the end of hunger in the United States and abroad.

Throughout this readable and useful book, two things should be noted. First, the Action Steps that punctuate each of the chapters progress from prayer through interlinked steps of study, financial giving or stewardship, connecting with the impoverished, ritual, advocacy, and politics. They enable Christians and fellow travelers to be the *Ambassadors of Hope* (Robert Seiple) that we are called to be. This is a path of committed discipleship marked out by a prophetic vision of justice (Isaiah 58:6-14), by works of compassion (Matt. 25:31-45), also central to our theological identity.

Second, there is more to the argument: 1) The question of *poverty and hunger* draw us to consider all persons in the image of God; 2) Reducing *child mortality* calls us to reflect on the incarnation, that our hope came as a child; 3) Promoting *gender equality* draws us to the mystery of unity and diversity, gender, ethnicity and race; 4) The goal of achieving *universal primary education* reminds us that education, schools and universities, has been a gift of the Church to western culture; 5) Improving *maternal health* reminds us that the health of the mother is key to the health of the community; 6) The work of combating *HIV/AIDS, malaria, and other Diseases* drives us to ask whether calamity/suffering is payback for sin; 7) The task of ensuring *environmental sustainability* calls us to be not only "stewards of the mysteries of God" (Col.1:9) but also "stewards of the earth" (Gen. 2:15); and 8) developing *networks for development* raises the question of those with whom we will associate, to issues of "exclusion and embrace."

What can one person do? Our authors remind us that eliminating poverty and its related problems is God's work. In this we can see God reaching out across our boundaries. God is drawing all things into God.s self, calling us to take part in this work. We are not in this alone. *So, what can one person do?* Ask Paul Farmer or Gloria White Hammond. Ask Bob Seiple and Jimmy Carter. Ask Bono. We can join hands with the work being done, work initiated by God, work that is already going on. Together, we can collaboratively make a difference in the world around us. This is the "liturgy after the liturgy"–a word of hope for human flourishing in a century that needs a fresh vision of mission.

## 38.
## *Strategies for Holistic Mission:*
## *An "Emergent" and Emerging Church*

By Rodney L. Petersen
Boston Theological Institute

The *Antioch Agenda* provides a vision for holistic mission for an *emerging church* in the 21st century. Such vision places ethical accent on living in the present in a context marked by the Book of Acts against an historical backdrop of biblical witness. Biblical revelation has always been deemed to have a prophetic role in the sense of a challenge to right living. To whatever extent it offers insight on global politics–events preceding an envisioned return of Christ (pre-millennialism in various forms), bound up with it (amillennialism), or overcome through the progressive energies of history (post-millennialism)–ethics trumps eschatology in Christian theology.

There have been many different paradigms and ways for doing mission, for allowing the good news of Jesus Christ to shape lives and social structures. Mission has taken on specific strategies with defined objectives in relation to different models of history, but always with the end in view of forming disciples of Christ. This is the case for each of the great periods of mission and preaching: the early expansion of the church, the preaching of reform by late medieval mendicants and new urban orders, Hussite, Protestant and Catholic re-formations, periods of mission and revival in the same groups and among the Orthodox. And mission today requires a sense of history. It requires confidence that God through Christ is destroying the powers of oppression, alienation, sickness, and death (I Corinthians 15: 22-28), that strength is given the church to do God's mission (Romans 5:3-5) and that the end in view is good (Revelation 21).

A strategy for holistic mission begins with theological self-understanding. The development of such a strategy is the intent of the *missional church movement.* Darrell Guder who has given guidance to this perspective develops the thesis that Christian mission in regions like the United States or Europe, "is fraught with *theological* ambiguity." This ambiguity grows out of the unique histories of these regions and also out of challenges to whether mission is conceived of as method or theology, as constitutive of several tasks to be undertaken by the church or as shaping the church's core identity. For Guder, the tragedies of conflict, genocide and holocaust through the twentieth century have deepened the theological question of the nature of valid mission even as they have brought its necessity universally to our consciousness and created the need for a missional ecclesiology.

The *"Emergent"* and *emerging church movement* is developing in relation to this missional conversation, a 21st Christian church whose participants seek to engage postmodern people, especially the unchurched with a missional approach to Christianity so as to reshape belief, standards and methods to fit contemporary realities. Scot McKnight identifies five themes within this trend: such a church seeks to be *prophetic, postmodern, praxis-oriented, post-evangelical and political* (*Christianity Today,* January 19, 2007). Eddie Gibbs and Ryan Bolger (*Emerging Churches: Creating Christian Community in Postmodern Cultures,* Baker, 2005), offer a definition of the movement that defines "emerging" in this way: as those who practice "the way of Jesus" in the postmodern era.

What might education look like in terms of an "Antioch Agenda" for an *emerging church*? Elizabeth Conde-Frazier of Clermont and Robert W. Pazmiño of Andover Newton write about a vision for such prompted by the work of Orlando Costas whereby the entire church is caught up in the liberating news of the gospel. They cite Costas' use of Hebrews 13:12-13: "Therefore Jesus suffered outside the city gate in order to sanctify the people by his blood. Let us then go to him outside the camp and bear the abuse he endured." For Conde-Frazier and Pazmiño, the implications of drawing such diversity into the church affect the structures of leadership; it creates a church that is inclusive of cultural difference and promotes educational policies that are as informative as they are transformational.

A missional context for the emerging 21st century church is the global youth culture, shaped by different ways of engaging or expressing alienation from the dominant culture. Ken Johnson of the Seymour Institute relates the hope of the gospel for urban youth, often sensitive to the destructive powers of oppression, finding voice in Hip-Hop culture and its music. Increasingly disseminated among all youth, with global reach through media and other methods and systems, Thug Life and its variations define an alternative worldview with religious implications. For Johnson, this is a formidable urban border that contemporary missions must cross and for which a credible and up-to-date Christian apologetic is needed.

The twentieth century is noted for populations in movement: war, ethnic cleansing, economic and political unrest and ecological disaster have combined to create an unparalleled human crisis of immigrants, refugees and asylum seekers that continues into the twenty-first century. An *emerging church* with an *Antioch Agenda* recognizes this demographic reality. Ruth Bersin, Director of the Refugee Immigration Ministry, describes this area of "border crossing" as she writes out of her extensive cross-cultural experience. Beginning with the Great Commission (Matthew 28:19-20) and the Great Commandment (Matthew 25: 34-40; cf. 22:37), she looks at mission through the lens of family systems theory and stresses the need to foster relationships that neither project our fears nor scapegoat that which is other and different.

Christian mission is good news for all, but especially for the poor and marginalized. This aspect of social healing is expressed in different social and national settings. Daniel Jeyaraj of Andover Newton and the Church of South India finds useful lessons from the history of Christian missions in the work of Christian Frederick Schwartz (1726–1798) which can be applied cross-culturally. Issues of restorative justice as marked out by Mennonite scholar Howard Zehr, Boston University's Tom Porter and Episcopal Divinity School's Ed Rodman carry a restorative and redemptive theme to our overburdened prisons, myriad social issues and including the scourge of racism and the practice of slavery as it continues in our world today.

That social healing can come even in areas of racial and ethnic hatred is exemplified in the work of Boston College's Raymond Helmick, S. J. Such conflict, often engineered by cynical manipulative forces playing on group anxiety and historical grievance, make of religion a weapon for harm rather than healing. Helmick writes out of his missional motivation of the ways he has been guided to find reconciliation in the most intransigent of conflicts. His analysis of the dynamics within majority and minority groups, the direct nature of a conflict and the framework within which it occurs can yield solutions. Often *scapegoating* is fundamental to conflict in ways that mandate the need for understanding, and call for the potential of forgiveness in order to find reconciliation. He adds that the spirit of these conflicts seems to have become more cataclysmic following the 9/11 attack as the United States appeared to also be overcome by its own fear and rage.

Youth alienation, populations under stress, the needs of the poor and marginalized, racial and ethnic hatred and discrimination – all these form contexts for Christian mission in an *emerging church* with an *Antioch Agenda*. They are areas of social disease that find prophetic direction (Isaiah 58:6-14; Matthew 25:34-45) as Christian disciples discover the courage to be the body of Christ in the world, "stewards of the mysteries of God" (Col. 1:9); but Calvin DeWitt, President emeritus of the Au Sable Institute of Environmental Studies, challenges us with more: to be "stewards of the earth" (Gen. 2:15). Creation, too, is recipient of God's mission as the whole *cosmos* looks for liberation through the gospel (Romans 8: 18-21); personal and social salvation are only an aspect of the deeper ecological healing that is required of us and of our world. DeWitt draws attention to the interplay between the biosphere and missiology as he places importance upon putting our contemporary scientific understanding of the world into interactive relationship with missiology. This holistic mission is every Christian's vocation. We are reminded of this by Weston Jesuit School of Theology's Margaret Eletta Guider, OSF as she argues before the American Society of Missiology that we now live in a world where the distinctions between mission senders and mission receivers are blurred by our mutual dependencies.

The *Antioch Agenda* for an *emerging church* in the 21st century is an agenda that involves all peoples in the proclamation of the good news of Jesus Christ. It is an agenda that finds specific focus in the pressing issues of our day. These issues can be said to be the following four areas: 1) the need for human flourishing, 2) the demands of reconciliation in specific settings, 3) an affirmation of religious freedom in the context of a dialogue among religions, and 4) the necessity of freedom from fear.

The Millennium Development Goals (MDGs) offer a vision of human flourishing. Defined by the United Nations, they form a template for action. The lens of Christian reflection offers missional perspective: the goal of eliminating extreme *poverty and hunger* draws us to consider how all are made in the image of God; that of reducing *child mortality* calls us to reflect on the incarnation, that the embodiment of Christian hope came into the world as a child; promoting *gender equality* draws us to reflect on the mystery of unity and diversity – that of gender, ethnicity and race; the goal of achieving *universal primary education* reminds us that education, schools and universities, have been the gift of the Church to global cultures; improving *maternal health* reminds us that the health of the mother is key to the health of the community; the work of combating *HIV/AIDS, malaria, and other Diseases* drives us to ask whether calamity/suffering is payback for sin; the task of ensuring *environmental sustainability* calls us to stewardship; and developing *networks for development* raises the question of those with whom we are willing to associate, to issues of "exclusion and embrace" (Miroslav Volf). Mission in the twenty-first century fosters human flourishing.

Second, the *Antioch Agenda* for an *emerging church* in the twenty-first century is about reconciliation. Reconciliation, accompanied by forgiveness, grounded in justice–these all are central to Christian spirituality and open the gates forward to the repair of the world (*tikkun olam*). Robert Schreiter, CPPS calls attention to the vertical, horizontal and cosmic aspects of reconciliation. In work for the Conference on World Mission and Evangelism of the World Council of Churches (Athens 2005), he outlines six aspects of the reconciliation and healing: truth, memory, repentance, justice, forgiveness and love. Reconciliation begins in particular settings and reaches out to cosmic dimensions. If there is a role for reconciliation in the political realm (e.g., as assumed in the work of Gopin, Hehir, Helmick, Hollenbach, Lederach, Little, Petersen, Shriver, Volf, etc.), it finds its deepest grounding in theological reflection on God's work in Christ. This is where cycles of revenge and release are first encountered within a movement toward health and wholeness. Reconciliation involves, to use the words of Samuel Escobar, "Transforming Service." It is the "liturgy after the liturgy," to adopt the expression of Orthodox theologian Ion Bria.

Third, the *Antioch Agenda* for an *emerging church* assumes and promotes religious freedom. There is a growing sense across the globe that rights and obligations arise from the people as embodied in the *Universal Declaration of Human Rights* set forth by the United Nations (1948). This was given further significance for religious consciousness and liberties in the U.N.'s *Declaration on the Elimination of All Forms of Intolerance and of Discrimination Based on Religion or Belief* (25 November 1981). The social reality of people migrating around the world, contemporary technology and media – as well as an increasing tendency to standardize national citizenship – have all promoted a sense of global citizenship. With this has come an increasing understanding of the necessity for a dialogue among religions (e.g., as in the work of Esposito, Küng, Smock, etc.) in the context of the freedom of religion. Religious citizenship takes shape around issues of identity, lifestyle, specific needs and networks. Just as Christianity played a role in globalization through the democracy of salvation, fostering global religious freedom in the context of a dialogue among religions must also be affirmed as a mission goal so as to promote the authenticity of religious choice and commitment.

A fourth goal laid out in an *Antioch Agenda* for an *emerging church* in the twenty-first century is to promote freedom from fear. At another time and place Franklin Delano Roosevelt offered a vision of a world founded upon four essential freedoms: the freedom of speech, freedom of religion, freedom from want, and the freedom from fear. This must also be a dimension of mission in the twenty-first century. "Do not fear" is the charge given to Abraham, alike to Joshua, then with resonances through Jesus to John's vision, the Apocalypse: "Be strong and courageous... I will be with you" (Deuteronomy 31-23). The monotheistic faiths tell us that we live in a world of the one God, upon whose goodness we can totally rely. The victory cry of the Lamb who was slain is that, "He will wipe away every tear from their eyes. There will be no more death or mourning or crying or pain, for the old order of things has passed away" (Revelation 21:4).

# 39.
## Theological Voices Reflecting the New Antioch

By Rodney L. Petersen
Boston Theological Institute

**M**ission in the 21st century will be a topic of much discussion: What is it? Why is it done? The Book of Acts tells the story of the first commissioning of missionaries out of Antioch (Acts 13:1), noting the context as that of prophets and teachers fasting and gathered for worship and prayer. Strengthened with spiritual power, Barnabas and Saul (Paul) were perceived through the Spirit to be called and set apart for a special mission, a first missionary journey to the dark continent of Europe. Strengthened with spiritual power, the three prophets and teachers remaining in Antioch, Simeon called Niger, Lucius of Cyrene and Manaen, lay their hands on the two departing ones, indicating by their names that at least two of the three may have been African in origin.

While the gospel is embedded in Judaism, this scene and the events it portrays in Acts chapters 13-14 carry us to a first council of the church at which issues of gospel and culture are preeminent, the Jerusalem Council (Acts 15:1-35), to be the early church's first cultural crisis, occasioned by Antioch and its missionary aftermath. The decision reached: one did not have to become Jewish before becoming a follower of Jesus.

We stand today on the point of another cultural crisis, a "clash of civilizations"–and we are learning that we do not need to become "western" before becoming Christian. The first chapter in the forthcoming book, The Antioch Agenda, by Charles Onyando Oduke, S. J., "Listening to Voices Outside Our Gate," reminds us of this. Oduke asks us to perceive, through the lens of the destruction of the U. S. World Trade Center and Pentagon (September 11, 2001), a larger world, one in which local and international actions interpenetrate. The language of contemporary political reference, use of antiquated or demeaning sociological terms such as, "third world" perpetuates historical myopia, lacks social realism and conveys disrespect. Mission requires global partnerships and networking toward the healing of the world. Christian mission requires, in Oduke's opinion, the perspectival outlook of "cosmopolis," an idea advanced by Bernard Lonergan, which rejects the "screening of memories.., the falsification of history...." We are at an historical moment which requires us to listen to the cry of the citizens of the world: "Listening to voices outside one's gate is a humble admission for the need for all cultures to complement one another."

One way to listen to voices "outside one's gate"–whether this be Africa, Asia, Europe, the Americas or the Pacific – is to recognize that God speaks all languages. Using the work of the 19th century Hindu convert to Christianity, Indian nationalist, journalist and theologian, Brahmabandhav Upadhyay (1861-1907), Gordon-Conwell's missiologist Timothy Tennent asks us in, "Listening to Voices Outside the Gates," to take note of not only the linguistic translatability of the Christian message, but its *cultural* translatable nature as well. Not only does the gospel come to us as an enscripturated text, but also as an encultured message. It must be made intelligible in specific, local contexts. Drawing on the work of Orlando Costas, authentic theology is "reflecting on the faith in the light of one's historical context." Upadhyay sought to use the language of *advaitic* Hinduism as an interpretive bridge to better communicate Christianity to enquiring Hindus.

In "Beyond Huntington's Gate: Orthodox Social Thinking for a Borderless Europe," Marian Simion writes about how the end of global bipolar conflict has impacted the Orthodox churches in their encounter with society, particularly as European political theory experiences the end of the Grotian [Hugo Grotius] statist model. A challenge of globalization is the need to revisit the Kantian universalistic model, but in alliance with Christian universalism–"no more Jew or Greek": politically, in order to shape Europe's new identity and perhaps that of the wider family of nations; theologically, to make space for the churches to exercise their prophetic role. This is challenging not only for Europe, but also for North America as pointed out by John B. Kauta, "Is North America a Mission Field? What Does the World Church Say?"

Our journey through the book, *Antioch Agenda*, asks us to move, "Outside Many Gates," as mission today mandates many conversations. This is to continue Paul's dialogue with society as revealed in his Letters, theologian Mark Heim's intent as he documents four "conversations" in

Orlando Costas' life that shape methodology: "Just as the Macedonian call to Paul had been the means by which the gospel passed into the European world, Orlando saw this call as one by which the renewed gospel might come again to the dominant European culture of North America, where (as he put it) the North American Hispanic community and other racial minority communities were '"the bridge between mainstream North America and the peoples on the periphery of the world.'" These conversions were brought to an agenda for the churches that included the internal horizons of universality, ecumenism and world Christianity, and gave attention to three external horizons, "critical literacy" in religion, the scientific cast of culture, and the universality that is constituted by the world religions.

In "Between the Gates," Samuel Solivan reflects on Costas' many roles as evangelist, educator and mission analyst–taking the gospel to the crossroads of contemporary life, theology "between the gates" of life that mark the boundaries of political, economic, religious or social acceptability. Here Costas' methodology exemplifies what Miroslav Volf identifies as crossing boundaries of "exclusion and embrace." Costas sought conversation partners from different contexts and between different sets of borders or boundaries, breaking open the intramural conversations that often dominate theological reflection and missional action.

Listening beyond the gates takes each of us into the realm of the other, an important move toward the maturation of identity. The gospel has long been in the thrall of European and North Atlantic culture, but for all the good that has come of this, it is not an unmitigated blessing. It has come with a price. That price has been increasingly set by the political and economic power residing in transnational corporations and in the technology that shapes perception, captivates the imagination, and offers legitimacy to current consumerist and other practices.

Listening "outside" and "beyond" our gate asks us to take up participation in global community, rejecting what Robert Bellah identified as an "ontological individualism," a failure to see how we are embedded in a deeper social ecology where individual interests are linked to the common good. The restoration of social ecology must be one of the goals of Christian mission, lending both meaning and authenticity to mission. Global community requires that we see ourselves as global citizens. Few have been as tireless in promoting such an idea as Quaker peace activist Elise Boulding, a cause taken up by the former president of Notre Dame University, Theodore M. Hesburgh. There can be no place for discrimination or social and economic exclusion from the perspective of global citizenship, no priority given to corporatism, cultural dominance or any perspective that promotes benign or lethal forms of dependency.

Global consciousness has been driven by mission, not just by corporatism and technology–and it is important to ask who has been in the driver's seat. Leslie Sklair and colleagues have argued that global capitalism driven by politically connected transnational corporations drive the culture. This may be, but as the rise of global Fundamentalism illustrates, the picture is not always so clear. Of the five categories of persons that political scientist Richard Falk identifies as engaged with global needs and networks–global reformers, elite global business people, global environmental managers, politically conscious regionalists, and trans-national activists–four of the five have grassroots activism at their core. In his later discussion of globalization, Falk makes the distinction of globalization from above and from below, the former being economistic and often brutal in nature and the latter oriented to global human rights, often alive in relation to living religious traditions. Legitimacy for such activism is not drawn from any state, whether in areas of global economics, environmentalism, human rights, but from a kind of natural law although seldom identified as such. The connection made between globalization and mission by Boston University's Dana Robert, earlier in this volume, Antioch Agenda, now becomes clearer.

If the Christian movement gains legitimacy from universalism associated with a kind of "natural law," it also finds this through its expression of local culture. Both are implied in Andrew Walls' work. Local cultures become caught up in a larger Christian movement to the extent that they can be articulated through theology. The International Missionary Council (Jerusalem, 1930) stressed that the Christian message must be expressed in national and cultural patterns, implying movement beyond Euro-North American cultures. This indigenization was furthered by the Theological Education Fund in the 1970s with its emphasis upon contextualization. Decolonization in political and mental sovereignty, signaled by the Liberation and then Pentecostal theologies of Latin American, offered legitimacy to an array of theologies–water buffalo theology (Thailand), minjung theology (Korea), and other national theologies throughout Asia as well as to such rapidly growing movements as African Initiated Churches (AICs) and indigenous theologies. Examples such as these offer opportunities for debate as charges of syncretism, accommodation, situational and biblical fidelity have vied with one another through phases of adaptation, incarnation, and self-conscious identity formation.

Local theologies have permitted the expression of suppressed identities through affirmation of an inherent human dignity. Group consciousness, histories of privilege and depravation – as well as local languages and folk ways – crowd together to shape these identities–and identity has political implications. The Christian movement, growing worldwide, struggles to find the way through these complexities of gospel and culture to "integral mission," affirming, perhaps, what Kwame Appiah calls, "rooted cosmopolitanism." We are told in the text to "fix our eyes on Jesus" (Hebrew 12:2), yet we are more aware than ever of how differently he may be depicted. But he is the one–prophet, priest and king–who gives identity to the church and gives the church courage to be the body of Christ in the world.

# 40.
# *An Advent Reflection: New Means for Mission*

By David Dawson, Presbytery of Shenango; &
Charles West, Princeton Theological Seminary

As we approach the centennial celebration of the Edinburgh Missionary Conference of 1910, significant for the social movements which descended from it–not least of which is the World Council of Churches–the following question was asked by David Dawson (current President of the American Society of Missiology–EF):

Christian mission has been advanced through a variety of agencies. William Carey spoke of this as "using means." What is the present experience (seen in the context of historical patterns) of mission agency? What questions need to be considered by those wishing to look critically at mission agency?

His question (drawing from Andrew Wall's chapter "Missionary Societies and the Fortunate Subversion of the Church" in *The Missionary Movement in Christian History*, Orbis, 1996, pp. 241 – 254) intended what is presently happening in ecumenical-evangelical-Roman Catholic denominational structures and congregations, the broader theological/ missiological issues and particularly the question of the ecumenical integrity of mission. This question elicited the following reply from Charles West (Professor Emeritus of Christian Ethics, Princeton Theological Seminary).

Dear David,

This comes to you from the stimulus of the Mission History Group that meets every so often at the Presbyterian Historical Society in Philadelphia. We're old-timers, with memories and a few ideas. Don Black convenes us. The meeting this week included David and Elisabeth Gelzer, Eileen Moffett,

Connie Thurber, Sue Althouse (formerly of Japan), Margery Sly of the Historical Society and myself.

I remember that at the end of the Eastern Fellowship meeting of the American Society of Missiology early this month you appealed for help in organizing next year's meeting around the theme: mission and church structures. Am I right? If so, we were on your wavelength. We all know the confusion in the Presbyterian Church about this. Other denominations have the same problems. And we are surrounded by all kinds of mission initiatives related to congregations, independent churches, or to no church at all. Well, here are some thoughts on the subject. They are my own, though they are inspired by, and grow out of our discussion in Philadelphia this week. I'm copying it to the group.

First, there was, in the decades following Edinburgh 1910, a vision of the Church in ecumenical mission. We felt it; we were inspired by it, and we were drawn together from all confessions, in serving it. It was a growing and deepening vision. Learning repentance for our cultural, political and economic pride was part of it, as we grew into a community of churches worldwide bearing witness to the judging and redeeming grace of Christ for us all and for the world. We challenged and argued with each other. We agonized over our divisions. But we were in the same enterprise, learning with each other to serve the same lord, confident in the same reality and energized by the same hope. It was expressed in our church by the Commission on Ecumenical Mission and Relations and in our faith by the Confession of 1967.

Strange things have happened since then to this vision, for example: There have been digressions that have obscured it. One still risks making people angry by pointing them out. So be it. On the left the dry arose: the church is event not institution. There is truth in this, but the pursuit of it led to questioning every form of existing church. The church should lose and find itself in transforming or revolutionary action in the world, finding those points at which God's judgment challenges the powers that be and enables the poor and oppressed in their struggle to be free. A valid secular project, but a digression from mission because it does not speak to the whole of the human predicament, or offer the whole of the gospel.

And on the right, self-righteous individualism has emphasized the personal experience of salvation to the exclusion of the reign of the risen Christ in the world. Such people don't realize what a culturally limited American experience it often is! Small wonder that their digression tends to sanctify the social status-quo, and that their missionary practice perpetuates the old sending-receiving pattern: Once again the misuse of mission for a human end.

To this let me add another change, secular but not outside the realm of divine Providence: the quickening pace of life. In my parents' (your grandparents') day one traveled by ship, three weeks to a month, to one's field, and one stayed there seven years. At best one immersed oneself in the language and culture of the people to whom one was sent, and became, as a missionary, a person of two cultures. Today one can be home from Yaounde or Chiengmai in 24 hours. Each culture is caught up in global communications and economy. How does one become a cross-cultural missionary, a servant of the church universal in such a world? What should be the pattern of interchurch relations, as we share in our common mission? So where are we now?

1. Ecumenical work in mission goes on, including all sorts of people who wouldn't let the word ecumenical pass their lips. The American Society of Missiology is the most ecumenical organization to which I belong! Serious discussions among Roman Catholics and Protestants both ecumenical and non-ecumenical have produced deeper mutual understanding and inspiring common statements. There is often cooperation in the cultures and societies where the church is growing.

2. Christianity is proliferating in many parts of the world, in ways that defy any attempt to categorize or structure. One need only mention Pentecostalism in Latin America, indigenous churches in Africa, or the megachurches, independent churches, or Pentecostal churches in the USA. Traditional churches are losing ground, and their place is being taken by Christianity without any ecumenical form at all. How do we discern the work of the Holy Spirit in the midst of all of this? How can we serve the mission of God in this milieu? How are we one in Christ and what form should this unity take?

3. We need first of all, a new ecumenical vision of the church for the 21st century. That should come before any reconstruction of mission agencies or methods. The question facing mission today is the question of ecclesiology, in the very concrete form: how does Christ take form in and for the world we face today and tomorrow? Who are we, the body of Christ, as we confront and bear witness to the powers, the cultures, and the religions of the world? Let's not wait for a Mott, a Newbigin, or a D.T. Niles to answer that question. We can all work on it, in Louisville, in Princeton, in western Pennsylvania, or for that matter in Seoul, in Bangalore, or in Harare.

# 41.
# *Earthkeeping Ethic*

By Calvin B. DeWitt
University of Wisconsin at Madison

The oikoumene–the biosphere–owned by God, and now dominated by human beings, is the concrete situation of contemporary global missiology. In putting our contemporary scientific understanding of the world into interactive relationship with the understanding of missiology, as Orlando Costas and other missiologists envision, we can profitably address the topics of (1) witnessing to the concrete situations of life, (2) critical reflection, (3) analytic interpretation, (4) and obstacles and possibilities.

### *Witnessing to the Concrete Situations of Life*
Orlando Costas says that missiology has to do with Christian witnessing to the concrete situations of life. As we ask what this might include, we recognize clearly that this includes the concrete situations of people in whatever place or status they occupy: their home and habitat, food and spirit, joy and sorrow, justice and injustice. And in our day of global stewardship and knowledge of the nature of the biosphere and our relationship with it, it also includes the entire biosphere.

The biosphere has become part of our concrete situation. Ocean level rise may affect the area of floodplains covered by water and island communities may lose much or all of their land. Climate change may well alter the productivity of the land and settlement patterns of people. Deforestation may well change the climate and hydrologic cycle. Deforestation and habitat destruction also destroys extractive enterprises in harvesting native materials, nuts for consumption and oils, and flower petals for perfumes and fragrances.

Because connecting the local with the global is often difficult for the citizen and even the missionary locally, there is the need and also the capacity at the level of mission boards and agencies to connect with and to influence the issues and policies of regional and global stewardship, within these agencies individually and in collaboration and coalition with others, to work in accord to develop effective global responses and solutions. Work at the regional and global levels then can feed back to shape and re-shape the contributions at local levels that sum up around the world as improvements toward the global environmental situation—toward establishing the good news of the Kingdom of God locally and globally in lives and landscapes.

### Critical Reflection

Orlando Costas points to "critical reflection," in the "praxis of mission." In so doing he intends, as also do we, that missionaries and missiology need to be critically reflective upon what they are doing and accomplishing, both in the immediate and present situation, and at the regional and global levels on into the future. It is at these higher levels that missionaries and missiology, particularly in their institutions and agencies, foster the time, capacity, and must garner the resources for critical reflection and action, often well beyond those in the communities they serve.

In developing critical reflection at the local and agency levels, it can be very helpful to engage a framework of thinking that keeps three basic questions at the surface and continuously interacts with the questions and their answers informing each other:

First, there is the need for understanding, in critical reflection, how the world works in application to particular situations. This, of course, must include the immediate individual context but extends to embrace the wider contexts of community, region, soil and climate, and biosphere. In addressing how the world works, clearly there is need to immerse people into what is understood through the natural science about such things as the hydrological cycle, role of forests and vegetation in the landscape, the variety of living species, etc. But, this should go well beyond, as to include how people and communities work, how they interact with, contribute toward, and diminish the broader environments and contexts within which they operate, on through regional and continental levels, to the whole biosphere.

Second, in critical reflection, there is the need to develop a full understanding of what ought to be, at the individual, community, and global levels. What ought to be–the subject matter of ethics–evaluates what is happening in life and the environment with a concern for whatever it is that degrades individuals, communities, and the environment locally and globally needs to be responsibly and effectively addressed. Just doing things without reflecting upon whether these things and their impacts really ought to be is not acceptable, no matter how well-intended. What ought to be involves not only the things over which the missionary worker or community member has control but necessarily must deal with the wider society and environment, on up to the entire biosphere, and the various institutions that provide the incentives and constraints on the life of people and the land.

Third, is the need to consider practices as these are engaged in tending to our environments, providing food and shelter, processing wastes, transporting people and resources, and relating to sustaining these resources and the wider creation. Praxis is not simply a matter of doing something, but is wisely constrained by what we know and understand about how the world works and by the bounds by what we know and understand constitutes right living. For missiology, this recognizes that members of the community need to engage in practices of benefit to right living in the community, but also that they must do so with critical reflection in its broader regional and global aspects. Good practice locally might be found, upon its accumulation across a community, region, or the biosphere, detrimental to its larger contexts, and will need appropriate modification or replacement. Responsive missiology reflectively puts into regional and global contexts local praxis, and makes adjustments toward living rightly on earth at regional and global scales.

### Analytic Interpretation

Missiology, Costas tells us, involves analytic interpretation. This means that critical reflection engages the best analytical thinking and methods to address the needs for a vital and refreshing missiology. It is critical reflection that involves evaluation and projection, again with a depth of thought that goes well beyond a reflective entry into the missionary journal. And this in turn is directed to "the meaning, effectiveness, obstacles and possibilities" for communicating the Gospel—the Good News—to the world.

By reflecting upon the meaning of the Gospel here, we can fruitfully consider the definition of Wayne C. Booth of religion as "the passion to live rightly and spread right living." The Gospel message, so clearly and convictingly presented in the Gospels, is passionate. It is passionate toward living rightly—toward right living on earth. It also is passionate for spreading right living. Passionate missiology necessarily works to preach, teach, and model right living. Passionate missiology seeks to spread right living across communities and cultures, thereby bringing good news to every creature.

### Obstacles and Possibilities

As we are advised by Costas to evaluate and project obstacles and possibilities of communicating the Gospel to the world, we confront an expression that is perhaps our greatest obstacle. It is the wide-spread proclamation, "Well, you have to look out for number one!" Remarkably, at least in scriptural contest, this proclamation defines "number one" as oneself. This expression, and its increasing incorporation across American society and around the world, represents one of the greatest obstacles to bringing good news to every creature, the biosphere, and the whole creation. It does, however, present a missiological opportunity, and this is its replacement, by missionary proclamation and witness with the expression, "Well, you have to look out for Number One.," Here, however, Number One means the Creator of heaven and earth to whom the earth and its fullness, the world and all who dwell therein, belong. Here, Number One means Jesus Christ, the one by whom all things (ta panta) are created, held together, and reconciled to God (Col. 1:15-20).

Neither the earth nor our own selves belong to us, in the biblical view. Instead the earth and biosphere belong to God. Moreover, all human beings also belong to God. This is our missiological comfort and it is God's ownership of the biosphere, and of ourselves, that opens our missiological opportunity. "Looking out for Number One," as central to the Gospel in our time, places Christian missions among the solutions for addressing the care of God's creation, even as it withdraws them as participants in degrading and destroying the biosphere. It brings corrective actions whenever and wherever needed, and moves with deep dedication to the practice of faithful earthkeeping in all of its many dimensions.

The concept of earthkeeping is derived from Genesis 2:15 where we read of God's expectation that Adam of adamah will *keep* the garden. The Hebrew word translated here as *keep* is *shamar*, and merits our careful attention. It is the same word used in the blessing of Aaron (Numbers 6:24): "The Lord bless you and *keep* you."22 This is a blessing that looks not for a preservationist keeping as would be indicated by the Hebrew word, *natsar*. Both *natsar*, and *shamar* are applied to keeping the Law, which must both be preserved and kept. Given the availability of both words, it is significant that shamar is the word used for keeping people and the garden. For people, it expects that God.s keeping will nurture human life-staining and life-fulfilling relationships with vibrant wholeness and dynamic integrity.social relationships with parents, mates, children, siblings, and neighbors; ecological relationships with land, air, water, and other creatures; and human relationship with God.

As in "peoplekeeping" so in "earthkeeping". Earthkeeping maintains and assures dynamic vitality, energy and beauty of the garden and its creatures. When informed by science, we know that keeping involves the fine balancing between constructive and destructive processes. In people and other vertebrate creatures it includes, for example, the dynamic reformation of the skeletal system of dynamic creatures in a dynamic world.

Osteoblasts build up bone where needed while osteoclasts tear it down where superfluous, in a highly controlled and finely-tuned process that maintains a strong skeletal system that yet responds to the needs of a changing body under changing stresses. In nature and creation it includes the dynamic re-formation of living systems from previously living systems in a dynamic biosphere. Photosynthesis builds up material and energetic resources energized by the sun while respiration and decomposition processes break down dead materials to energize and perpetuate species and ecosystems, controlled by constraints of material and energy budgets that sustains life as a flowing stream of biotic intricacy, complexity and biodiversity.

When people *keep* the garden and creation they do so in this deep, full, and dynamic sense. Reflecting God's keeping of them, they profess and confess in their very deeds and actions that the creatures under their care must be kept with dynamic integrity. They must be maintained and enabled to maintain their proper connections with members of their own kind, with the many other kinds with which they interact, with the soil, and with the air and water upon which they depend for their life and fruitfulness. They must even be maintained, in ways complementary to our scientific understanding of the world, within the trophic cycles of life and death and in energy and material transfers upon which the life of the biosphere depends. *As God keeps and sustains us, so must we keep and sustain the God's Creation.*

## 42.
# A Review of "God and Money"
# by Nimi Wariboko

Review By Norman Faramelli
Episcopal Divinity School & Boston University School of Theology

God and Money is an ambitious, insightful, and creative theological approach to the understanding of the international monetary economy. The book is significant for several reasons: First, it not only touches on an important subject, but it also demonstrates how theological language can help us understand the contemporary global monetary economy. Secondly, the book focuses on currencies as a way to understand the "center" of the global economy. Thirdly, the author, Nimi Wariboko, is deeply engaged in a creative effort to lay out the need for a new global currency – a currency designed to assist the poorer nations of the world, thus leading to greater global equality. Most impressive was the author's effort to use theological categories as a way to understand the inner workings of the currency system. In this respect, this book differs from other works that simply apply theological categories to contemporary issues.

God and Money is divided into two parts. Part one contains chapters on how to understand money through the lenses of theology by reviewing the socioeconomic interpretations of money, and by focusing on money as "social relation." Nimi Wariboko makes a compelling point that money is both a mode of social relation and a "relational-thing." Simply put, money is not just a mode of material exchange. Using Paul Tillich's category of "demons", in the second part of his book, Nimi Wariboko analyzes the distortions of monetary relations by looking at how money is a "center" of the global economic empire. The author then develops a Trinitarian model of the global monetary system and calls for the development of a common currency, (which he calls "the Earth Dollar"), indicating how such a currency could assist the so-called third world by serving as an antidote to global inequality.

One might easily be intrigued by Wariboko's use of the Trinitarian language in relation to the understanding of the current monetary situation and its reconstruction. He fully realizes that all historical attempts to understand the Holy Trinity are based on relationality, yet he does not engage any arguments surrounding the Holy Trinity, nor does he tap into the different understandings of the Trinitarian language today. Instead, he draws upon the work of two major theologians, Paul Tillich and Miroslav Volf. From Tillich, he borrows the three fundamentals of Trinitarian language: the dialectics of the absolute concretized in the idea of God, the dialectics of life, as it engages the ground of being, and the dynamics of depth, form and meaning. From Volf, the author employs the perichoretic sociality of the Trinity that is based on ecclesial models. ("Perichoresis" is the inter-penetration of the One and the Many.)

The genius of the book is that it takes philosophical abstractions and brilliantly makes them operational as to understand the international monetary system. Additionally, the author challenges the reader by demonstrating how a theological model can be used in the reconstruction of the monetary system. Nevertheless, the book is not just about theology. It is also an engagement with economists such as John Maynard Keynes and Robert Guttman. This interdisciplinary approach reflects the background, the experience and the knowledge of the author to engage in such an undertaking. Nimi Wariboko not only taught and worked in investment banking and financial analysis, but he is also an expert in social ethics and theology.

In several places, Wariboko attempts to avoid what theologian Bernard Lonergan called the "social ethicists' tendency to be content with 'vague moral imperatives' instead of figuring out moral precepts from the immanent intelligibility of economic processes." (p. 26) Instead, the author plunges into the understanding of the inner dynamics of the global monetary system, on how it functions, on the principles and values upon which it is based, and on the inevitable results of such a system. For example, one oucome of the current dynamics of the global monetary system is the way in which the dollar the euro and the yen shape the global economy to the disadvantage of the economies of poorer nations in Africa, Latin America and Asia. It is for this reason that Wariboko calls for a new global currency - the Earth Dollar – realizing nevertheless that the nations now profiting from the current situation will fiercely oppose its development and implementation. He also realizes that if China becomes the dominant global economic power, and if the yuan will replace the dollar, the euro and the yen as the dominant currencies, the yuan will still maintain similar forms of inequality. At the same time, Wariboko remains fully optimistic that the international monetary dynamics will unavoidably move the world toward a global currency.

In his analysis, Wariboko makes a compelling argument against the thesis introduced by Michael Hardt and Antonio Negri in their work *Empire* (Cambridge: Harvard University Press, 2000), where they argue that there is no "center" in the modern economic empire. Although Wariboko sometimes maintains the same argument like Hardt and Negri, he is very critical of their analysis (and other analyses of globalization), which fail to come to grips with the currency issues. For Nimi Wariboko, currencies are the "center".

Wariboko cites the numerous advantages of the Earth Dollar. These include the democratizing of the international monetary systems and the global economy, the democratizing of the world resource use, giving the poor countries more control over their own national resources, and reducing dependency on the international economy. Additionally, the Earth Dollar will provide a mechanism for equitable distribution of adjustment burdens, and will address issues of rapid fluctuations in foreign exchange rates. Above all, the Earth Dollar addresses the fundamental problems of inequality between poor and rich nations. (p. 235)

Just to return to the Trinity model, in analyzing the current monetary economy and also in constructing an alternative currency, Nimi Wariboko utilizes this model with its emphasis on both particularity and universality - the one and the many - which in its essence is a classical philosophical and theological problem. He wants to keep the diversity in currencies and the universality of the Earth Dollar in balance. Utilizing the concept of "perchoresis", he calls for an "indwelling of the Earth Dollar common to all of them that makes various national currencies into some sort of communion that be like unto the Trinity." (p. 214) Trinitarian concepts have never been easy to grasp, and this one is no different. It is important, however, that any model deals with both the particular and the universal - the One and the Many. And according to author, these concepts can be grasped without a full understanding of the theological issues surrounding the Trinity. Indubitably, there are difficulties in communicating theological concepts. Yet, what I find most impressive is that Wariboko shows the pragmatic value of these concepts.

It is also important to note that some of the secular views on economics, such as Adam Smith's "invisible hand," have deep roots in

John Calvin's understanding of the Divine Providence (pp. 34-36), a concept that can be traced back to Augustine, where one vice could be used to check another.

In conclusion, one might challenge Nimi Wariboko for claiming too much for the role of currencey in economic imperialism, while not dealing with other dimensions such as military power, media domination, global market monopoly, etc. Although this might be a justified challenge, in Wariboko's defense, it is alarming that some many critiques of globalization failed to recognize (or take seriously) the role of the monopoly of a few currencies (and their wild fluctuations), which can destroy the economies of poor nations and substantially increase their indebtedness. On a second note, one might also question whether the translation of theological concepts into empirical analysis flows as smoothly as the author implies.

In light of the recent financial meltdown, along with its global repercussions, it is clear that the role of the global monetary system needs to be taken more seriously. Furthermore, if one is concerned about fixing global inequalities, one may need to reflect over the idea of global currency. In this light, we can express our gratitude to Nimi Wariboko for calling these matters to our attention. It is a job well done.

## 43.
## *The Role of Forgiveness in Social Healing*

By Leonel Narváez Gomez
Foundation for Reconciliation, Bogotá, Colombia

Whenever a person is offended, three basic pillars of her life are deteriorated: significance, safety and socialization. The ungrateful memory of the offense keeps haunting the offended person (cognitive rehearsal) in such a way, that memory becomes the most difficult issue to be solved in case the person wants to embark in the process of forgiveness. If the offended person wants to journey towards reconciliation, then she has to make an additional effort to rebuild trust in the offender. Justice here, is not seen any more as a punitive act but rather as an effort to restore to offender.

The exercise of forgiveness and reconciliation becomes therefore, a heroic act, an expression of the highest spirituality and the best sign of total commitment to the reparation paradigm of the Gospel of Jesus. For too long Christianity has shamefully and poorly developed contents, methods and tools to strengthen the spirituality of forgiveness and reconciliation, which is the core of its message. In fact, theory and methods of forgiveness and reconciliation both in Christian tradition and in social sciences are still in its infancy.

The Fundación para la Reconciliación,(winner of the Honorable Mention UNESCO PRIZE Education for Peace -2006) born and based in Colombia, South America, has been promoting the ESPERE Program (Spanish acronym for Schools of forgiveness and reconciliation) based on strategies like the TOT Approach, Small Group therapy, Trauma management, and Step by Step method.

The Schools of F&R have been implemented primarily with victims and survivors of violence especially in poor areas of big cities like Bogotá, Sao Paulo, Rio de Janeiro, Mexico, Monterrey, Toronto, Boston, Santiago de Chile and other smaller cities. The training is offered in different environments like difficult schools, violent neighborhoods, prisons, church programs (where special contents are used to promote the ministry of reconciliation). Particularly enriching has been the exercise of forgiveness and reconciliation among ex-combatants of subversive groups in Colombia.

The ESPERE training is normally done in two stages: one stage for forgiveness and another for reconciliation. In the forgiveness stage the main topics are: forgiveness and un-forgiveness, decision to forgive, looking with different eyes, exercising compassion. In the reconciliation process the main issues are: justice, truth, pacts, reparation and celebrations. The contents of the course try to balance 4 essential dimensions of human beings: cognitive, behavioral, emotional and spiritual. The training uses rituals, symbols, psychodramas, songs as essential part of the methodology. Forgiveness is not only a powerful exorcism against violence but also and specially, it is a paradoxical expression of what a human being is called to be: homo reparans! The homo sapiens has been the cause of many wars, deaths and suffering.

The paradox of the Christian message and perhaps, the deepest meaning of being a human person, is not so much that we have to forgive and reconcile, but above all that we have to practice vicarious reparation. Indeed: we are constantly called to repair the inevitable limitations of other human beings! It is the philosophy of care and compassion! It is spirituality at its best!

## 44.
## *Life Together*

By Rodney L. Petersen
Boston Theological Institute

I am very grateful to you for your confidence in me in granting me the Forrest L. Knapp 2008 Ecumenical Award. When I was first asked to work as executive director of the Boston Theological Institute, and with the encouragement of the late George H. Williams, I had been working in Europe – and on occasion in southeast Europe – and was reluctant to trade one Balkan setting for another. As a self-acknowledged evangelical and "ecumenical" I was also tired to taking shots from both directions. Nevertheless, all of these contexts and others have impressed upon me the importance of our *life together*. With this as a title to my remarks I would like to share a few thoughts with you.

You will recognize this title as that of the remarkable book by Dietrich Bonhoeffer, written in 1938 after the Nazis closed down the clandestine seminary in Finkenwald (Pomerania) which he and others had created in 1935 for the training of young pastors. It is a book that reads like one of Paul's letters, giving ractical advice on how *life together* in Christ can be sustained in com munity. Its focus on the role of prayer, worship, work, and Christian service has become the bedrock of many renewal groups and *emerging* churches.

This is an appropriate book to reread as we enter 2008, a year of significant ecumenical anniversaries. This year marks the 100th anniversary of the Week of Prayer for Christian Unity, faithfully upheld by the Graymoor Friars – and, locally, by the Massachusetts Council of Churches. It is also the 60th anniversary of the World Council of Churches and 40th anniversary of our consortium, the Boston Theological Institute. December 8 will see the

60th anniversary of the United Nations *Universal Declaration of Human Rights.*

All of these anniversaries drive us to ask about the nature of human community, *life together*, easily beset by tribal animosity, whether in Kenya or with fresh potential in US Elections. Bonhoeffer emphasizes the spiritual nature of Christian community, i.e., community through and in Jesus Christ. To clarify the nature of this community he contrasts it with community as an ideal type and community as a psychological state. Bonhoeffer contends that Christian community is not an abstract Ideal but a divine reality. We are bound together by God in Christ. The process, document and decisions around *Baptism, Eucharist and Ministry* (*BEM*, 1982) say that all baptized in the name of the triune God are a part of one fellowship. There is no re-baptism among Christians. To reverse this ecumenical process is to step back in time and away from Christ. So also, the church is not merely a psychological state of mind. Bonhoeffer explains, "Because Christian community is founded solely on Jesus Christ, it is a spiritual and not a psychic reality" (31). According to Edmund Schlink, the focus on Christ, not on separate church organizations, carries us beyond the phenomena to the foundational (*Ökumenische Dogmatik*, 1983; cf.*The Vision of the Pope* 2001). This is a triumph of *agapé* over *eros.*

*So where are we today, sixty years later with respect to ecumenism?*

The epochal ecumenical document, *BEM*, has been followed by advances in bi-lateral relationships, such as the Formulas of Agreement of 1997 and the Augsburg Accord of 1999 between Rome and the World Lutheran Federation on justification. There have been significant advances in evangelical-ecumenical relationships and evangelical-Roman Catholic dialogue. Rome and Constantinople continue a kind of courtship while "grassroots" ecumenism has become the brand name for much of the *Emerging Church* movement, Pentecostalism and charismatic trailings. The World Council of Churches continues its flagship role, albeit through rough seas, by helping to birth the Global Christian Forum (Nairobi, 2007). Catholicism, Orthodoxy, the Anglican community, and the Protestant communions continue to chart competing courses oriented, largely, by differing conceptions of Ministry and with attention to Eucharistic detail, but not in denial of sixty years of progress. The Faith and Order Movement of the World Council of Churches has succeeded in anchoring discussion theologically around the document, *Confessing the One Faith.*

*An Ecumenical Explication of the Apostolic Faith as it is Confessed in the Nicene-Constantinopolitan Creed* (381). A Faith and Order Study Document, No. 153 (Geneva: WCC, 1991). The importance of "this relationship and of our relative unity" is underscored by Orthodox theologian Emmanuel Clapsis (*Orthodoxy in Conversation*, 2000, p. 8).

*So where are we today, sixty years later with respect to religion and human rights?*

The entire οἰκουμενη (oikoumene), "the inhabited world," has grown to recognize its defined planetary condition since 1946 when rocket-borne cameras gave us our first look at Earth from beyond the atmosphere. In another way, the privileged status of the United States was awakened to changing global realities by the attacks of September 11, 2001. Through these last sixty years the UN Declaration of Human Rights has been a kind of uneven leaven in human societies, augmented by the U.N.'s *Declaration on the Elimination of All Forms of Intolerance and of Discrimination Based on Religion or Belief* (1981). Religion, at times receiving the rap for human rights violations, has also grown as an interfaith movement, seeking mutual respect, toleration, and co-operation, following Hans Kung's lead, that there will be no peace in this world without a dialogue and peace among the world religions (Hans Kung, *A Global Ethic for Global Politics and Economics*, 1998). Through the proliferation of the global NGO movement since WWII, new patterns of religious networking have developed that allow particular religions to maintain their confessional stance while encouraging cooperative activity toward common ethical ends.

*Life together* as shaped by these ecumenical and inter-faith movements now finds itself defined by another agenda, that of planetary sustainability, made all the more precarious by destructive conflict.

There are many things that can diminish violence and enhance human security. The socio-psychological movement that has emerged around forgiveness and reconciliation, signaled so clearly in South Africa with the TRC (1995), alerts us to certain possibilities. A component of such in the face of implicit cycles of revenge is raised by Bonhoeffer in *Life Together* as he moves from the foundations of Christian community to its practices, "The Day with Others." Surveying the disciplines of the Christian community, Bonhoeffer comes to the imprecatory Psalms. He writes that insofar as we are sinners and express evil thoughts in a prayer of vengeance, we dare not do so; insofar as Christ is in us, the Christ who took the vengeance of God upon himself, these prayers can be an unbroken, constant learning, accepting, and impressing upon the mind of God's will in Jesus Christ. They can help to re-humanize the other, important in ecumenical, inter-faith and resource-driven conflicts. The BTI experienced an example of this as, led by Rabbi Arnold Resnikoff of the US Navy Chaplaincy, we and 50 theology students representing Muslim and Christian traditions wrote laments for the violence that had overwhelmed the former Yugoslavia, drawing upon the imprecatory psalms (See former BC Professor Frank Sullivan's book, *The Tragic Psalms*, 1987). These students continued to communicate with one another across communal boundaries for several years after the event, building *life together.*

These are things that make for *life together* for us as well in 2008. Around them no election is needed. Councils of churches, like this one, can promote forgiveness and reconciliation, concepts that are central to what it means to be community – local community, faith community or member of the community of nations.